D0287638

CRASH BOOM!

CRASH BOOM!

MAKE A FORTUNE IN TODAY'S VOLATILE REAL ESTATE MARKET

GREG RAND

CAREER PRESS

Pompton Plains, NJ

Copyright © 2011 by Greg Rand

All rights reserved under the Pan-American and International Copyright Conventions. This book may not be reproduced, in whole or in part, in any form or by any means electronic or mechanical, including photocopying, recording, or by any information storage and retrieval system now known or hereafter invented, without written permission from the publisher, The Career Press.

CRASH BOOM!
EDITED BY NICOLE DEFELICE
TYPESET BY GINA HOOGERHYDE
Cover design by Rob Johnson/Toprotype
Printed in the U.S.A.

To order this title, please call toll-free 1-800-CAREER-1 (NJ and Canada: 201-848-0310) to order using VISA or MasterCard, or for further information on books from Career Press.

The Career Press, Inc.
220 West Parkway, Unit 12
Pompton Plains, NJ 07444
www.careerpress.com

Library of Congress Cataloging-in-Publication Data

Rand, Greg.
    Crash boom! : make a fortune in today's volatile real estate market / by Greg Rand.
        p. cm.
    Includes bibliographical references and index.
    ISBN 978-1-60163-175-6 -- ISBN 978-1-60163-651-5 (ebook) 1. Real estate investment--United States. 2. Real property--
Purchasing--United States. 3. House buying--Unied States. 4. House selling--United States. I. Title.

HD255.R27 2011

2010054598

For Dad.

ACKNOWLEDGMENTS

Thanks to the following people who made this maiden voyage possible: Marsha, Matt, Joe, Dan, and Arlyne, for giving me the freedom to pursue this; Paul Adler, for teaching me half of what I know about real estate investing; Mark Stevens, for convincing me that I am the "smartest real estate guy in America"; Vinny Pribish, Allene Reynolds, Dick and Gail Sullinger, Sebastian Parisi, Jimmy Bellarosa, Jack Harrington, Michael Stenger, Margaret McMillan, Frank Kessler, and Anne Kaminsky, for sharing their experiences of living through the Great Depression.

Finally, but most of all, Leah, Diana, and Patrick, for being my inspiration to think long-term.

CONTENTS

PREFACE

This book is about taking control of your financial future and getting wealthy as a real estate entrepreneur. We all know that the economy cycles. It goes up, down, and up again. From boom to crash, and back to boom again. Why do so many people miss the booms and suffer the crashes? Fear. Lack of knowledge. Lack of resources. Maybe just lack of a plan.

I have only three objectives here. First, you must truly grasp the inevitability of the coming boom. This doesn't mean you should trust that it is coming in the next two years, but it is coming. The best demonstration of an economic cycle is when history repeats itself, so we will take lessons from the original, the Great Depression itself, and show how predictable The Great Recession really was. Equally as predictable is the boom that will come next. Internalize the inevitability of the coming boom, and you will have the faith and fortitude to secure a financially abundant life by playing the next cycle like a pro.

Second, I will provide you with a detailed road map on how to create a real estate investment business, very big or very small, that does not rely on luck. Herein are the tried and true secrets of the professional real estate investment industry. Decades of experience and study have produced the principles and strategies contained in this book. You won't learn a gimmicky approach that has been invented by one investment "guru," but the wisdom of hundreds of successful investors at all levels.

My third objective is to get you to *take action*. Breakthroughs in life begin when you decide that it is all up to you. This economic crisis, while predictable and similar to the Great Depression, is also unique in the way that the housing market played a central role. It is true that this is a once-in-a-generation crisis. It is also true that this is a once-in-a-generation opportunity. It's time to focus on the other side of the coin.

Think for a moment about the times in your life when you had the benefit of hindsight, and you beat yourself up for not capitalizing on some financial trend that seemed so obvious in retrospect.

Did you miss Microsoft, Yahoo, Ebay, Google, Apple, *and* Facebook?

Did you buy real estate in the 1990s and ride the biggest part of the boom, or did you miss it?

Are you always in search of the next macro-trend that you can capitalize on? Well, you've found it. Not just any trend, but the biggest real estate gold rush in a generation.

Mark these words. You are here, right now, being confronted with the opportunity to play a major financial trend with near-perfect timing. We are at the starting point of the next real estate wave. Don't let yourself look back in five years and realize that you missed it.

Ask yourself this: what does it feel like to buy low? It is lonely and frightening, so read on and allow your confidence to be restored. Read on and open your mind to learning a business you've always wanted to master. Read on and get ready to ride the next wave. It could change your life.

This is the opportunity you've been waiting for. Seize it, and if not, don't blame me.

INTRODUCTION

The worst economic downturn since the Great Depression!

—Everyone

I am not an economist or a historian. Throughout my entire life, I have heard about the Great Depression, but never learned much about it. During the last few years, it has been conjured up by media figures, politicians, and neighbors at every backyard barbecue in America. I was never really convinced that the comparison was accurate. Sure, I heard everyone parroting Warren Buffet, saying that the economy was going to "go off the cliff" if the federal government didn't bail it out. Every night on the evening news, we all heard about how unemployment and mortgage defaults were skyrocketing, and that home values and consumer confidence were plummeting. This was an assault on consumer confidence like I had never seen in my life. But something wasn't quite right.

Could it be that the government was trumping up the catastrophe in order to get permission to take over everything it could? Is it possible that the media would intentionally drive up fear to get ratings? Would both really make things seem worse than they are so they could manipulate consumer sentiment and impact elections?

Was optimism really becoming politically incorrect? The answers are a resounding *yes*.

And then there was Apple, a company whose sales and stock were off the charts because they reinvented the Walkman. iPods (and iPhones, iPads, etc.) are undoubtedly the coolest toys we've ever had, but they are still toys. You can get an unbranded MP3 player for less than $100. You can get a portable CD player for $20 and use all your CDs instead of converting them to iPod-compatible content. And yet everyone I know has multiple iPods.

It wasn't just Apple that forces you to question the accuracy and intentions of the doomsayers. There were other experiences I was having that didn't make sense, such as trying to take my wife to a fancy restaurant for her birthday and not being able to get a reservation for two weeks, or waiting on lines at every ride at Disney World. These observations clearly did not jibe with the "collapse of the American way of life."

Nothing here is intended to play down the legitimate hardship this poor economy is causing. On the contrary, the intention is to shine some daylight on the perverse and cruel impact of irrational pessimism. I will attempt to make the case in this book that there is a very real economic force called *irrational pessimism* that is the *cause* of much economic hardship, not the effect. More people are unemployed because successful businesses are afraid to expand. More people are losing homes they can afford because they are underwater and believe their home will never appreciate again. People with job security are convinced they don't have it, and live in fear.

Irrational pessimism is one reason why today's situation runs so parallel to the Great Depression. What has become known as the Depression Mentality began in the 1930s as an emotional and psychological phenomenon that gripped the majority of the population and drove the economy deeper into depression. But it didn't grip everyone. There were people back then who had unshakable faith in a comeback and were able to act with courage and optimism as a result.

During the real estate boom of the 2000s, the majority of Americans believed the real estate market would go up forever. Now many believe that the real estate market will *never* come back! They believe that the experience of the Great Recession is the new reality, and they choose to ignore the experience of the prior 65 years. As Warren Buffet says, "Be fearful when others are greedy, and be greedy when others are fearful."

It is time to take control of your future, because there is no one else you can rely on. The first step in breaking loose from the stagnation of the Great Recession is to recognize that many people prosper in times like these and they all have one thing in common: fear is not a factor.

The second step is to listen to the voice inside you that questions the "experts." Learn for yourself what is really going on. Entrepreneurs can thrive in any environment because they are defined by their belief that there are opportunities all around them. They trust that they have the ability to learn new things in order to adapt and succeed in a changing environment. This book will show you that opportunities are all around you, literally. In the town where you live, the area where you work, and the place you go on vacation are diamonds hiding in plain sight. I will show you how professional investors find those gems, polish them, and build a fortune.

The research for *Crash Boom!* started in the 1990s when I first began interacting with professional real estate investors. These men and women have uncanny common sense, and a keen intuition about this asset class. There are plenty of books on real estate investing available, but none substitute for real-world experience. Every opportunity, every property, and every deal is different. It is truly an art form when executed with creative strategy. This is not the strategy of one investor, but the result of my study of many, and the core habits of the best.

Crash Boom! is accompanied by technology and tools that you will learn to use, which will enable you to analyze entire real estate markets and individual properties. You will evaluate yourself to determine the best kind of investment property for you, and devise a plan for financial independence. You will learn how to make large sums of money right now, and how to convert those short-term hits into generational wealth.

Before we delve into the "how" of real estate wealth, it's important to lay the foundation of "why now?". The experts are correct about one thing. This economic crisis is the worst since the Great Depression, and history is repeating itself at the most basic levels of human nature. Let's take a trip back to the Roaring Twenties when the American people, our government, and business leaders made the economy ill, and how bootstrapping entrepreneurship was the antidote.

1 | An Entrepreneur's Explanation of the Great Depression

It was Christmas, 1933, four years after Black Tuesday, which was a day of infamy in American History, and the official start of the Great Depression. Instead of gifts that Christmas, the focus was on food, shelter, a job, and...Wait!

You've already heard this story a million times. It would not be crass of you to stop reading. It wouldn't make you a callous person just because you didn't want to dwell on the sad reality of the Great Depression one more time. You could still sympathize with people who had it tough, then and now, but it doesn't mean you have to read any further.

But this is a different story; one that needs to be told. This book is about success despite deep economic downturns. There were people who succeeded during the Great Depression!

It's true that unemployment hit 25 percent during the Depression, which means three out of four people had jobs.

No one is denying that far too many people went hungry during the Depression. It's also true that the 1930s was the decade when movie theaters first popped up in every town in America.

There is no question that homelessness soared in the 1930s, and it's also true that radio first became widely available as an information and entertainment source at the same time. There is another side to this.

What Caused the Great Depression?

There are two forces that drive economic cycles: macro economics and consumer sentiment. Understanding how these forces interact can shed light on historical events, and help explain the economic circumstances we are living through today.

When World War I ended in 1918, optimism took hold. Soldiers came home. Business growth drove the economy upward, and personal prosperity flourished.

In the background, a debilitating economic situation was gaining momentum. At this point in American history, the agricultural industry was our nation's largest employer. American farmers dramatically increased production during the war to support the war effort and feed Europe. When World War I ended, American farms saw exports plummet as the demand overseas for American agricultural products took a dive.

In addition, a trade war began not long after the war ended, and America's largest industry was facing a massive reduction in demand for its products. The United States government's response to this was to attempt to cushion the blow of increased unemployment by subsidizing the agricultural industry. With classic government short-sightedness, they began to pay farmers to produce large amounts of food that no one would ever eat. Farm production was growing, creating a massive surplus of agricultural capacity. By the end of the 1920s, this excess capacity reached critical levels that threatened worldwide commodity prices.

The government was able to hold off the increase of unemployment temporarily, but they destabilized prices of agricultural products in the process. After a few years, it became clear that government subsidy was too expensive and was not a permanent solution, so the subsidies ended and the inevitable layoffs occurred.

With the world still in some disarray due to WWI, and governments adopting a protectionist posture, the trade war that began at the end of WWI intensified through the decade. What began with high tariffs, quotas, licensing requirements, currency restrictions, and other constraints on imports and exports had the unintended consequence of trade restraints and price controls at home. The governments of the world determined that they would control commerce in order to protect their respective economies. The impact on business productivity and growth was devastating, but not plainly visible until the crash of 1929.

On the consumer sentiment side of the coin, this was the Roaring Twenties The end of the war sparked a sense of optimism, which led to excessive living. A new age of prosperity had set in.

Land speculation became a favorite investment opportunity for people at all levels. In a letter an attorney wrote to his friend at the time, he said, "In my town, everyone is becoming a land baron. The butcher, the town doctor, and the barber have all begun to take options on parcels on the outskirts." What's especially interesting about this statement is that "options" were devices that allowed an investor to control a piece of real estate with very little money down. In addition, lenders began to offer "interest only" mortgages to help investors borrow as much money as they could. Does any of this sound familiar?

The stock market also saw unprecedented levels of investment. As the decade unfolded, more and more people were getting rich in the market as their friends and neighbors watched from the sidelines. A sense that prosperity was the new reality took root.

Herbert Hoover was elected president in 1928. In his acceptance speech for the Republican Party Nomination, he said, "We in America today are nearer to the final triumph over poverty than ever before in the history of any land. The poorhouse is vanishing from among us."

On the other side of the aisle, John Jacob Raskob, Chief Executive of General Motors and head of the Democratic National Committee, published an article entitled "Everybody Ought to Be Rich" in the *Ladies' Home Journal.*

The traditionally reasoned and slightly pessimistic halls of the Ivy League Economics departments fell into step. Irving Fisher, economist at Yale University, stated just four days before Black Tuesday, "The nation is marching along a permanently high plateau of prosperity."

Some professionals on Wall Street saw the new class of "amateur investors" as sitting ducks and manipulated the markets to their own benefit. Professionals would take large positions in company stocks in order to drive the price up by creating the impression among amateurs that something exciting was happening with the company. Then amateurs would buy the stock at elevated prices, and the price would inevitably fall back to its original level. Schemes such as this were outlawed years later with the formation of the Securities Exchange Commission (SEC), but the damage was done. The combination of irrational optimism, the rise of amateur investors, and manipulation by professionals caused the market to rise to an unsustainable level. We've learned since that every new regulation crated by the SEC is met with a new creative approach by the professionals to bilk the amateurs.

Consumer sentiment was irrationally optimistic, and seduced by pursuit of easy money through risky speculation. Simultaneously, the macro economic situation was destabilized by war debt, a massive drop in exports, government constraints on trade, and the resulting slow down in business.

Then came Black Tuesday—October 29, 1929. The realities of a rapidly deteriorating economy collided with the bursting of optimistic fervor. It is widely regarded that the crash of 1929 was not the cause of the Great Depression, but the first obvious sign of it. The stock market lost almost half of its value in the two months following Black Tuesday. The speculation party was over, and the stampede which was running in one direction for most of the previous decade did a 180-degree turn. Not just from "buy" to "sell," but from optimism to pessimism. In fact, the market rebounded to within 15 percent of its high by April 1930, just six months later, but the damage to the consumer psyche was done.

The government's response to the crash was to double down on the same policies that helped to set up the deteriorating economy in the first place. In June of 1930, the Smoot-Hawley Tariff was passed, raising tariffs on more than 20,000 imported goods. The goal of the tariff was to protect American jobs from foreign competition, but the result was retaliation by governments around the world. International trade screeched to a crawl at a time when businesses were already faltering, and consumers were already recoiling from spending and investment.

International markets of American autos, textiles, copper, silver, and wheat declined as much as 50 percent from previous years. The auto industry in particular dropped by 40,000 units in 1930 and resulted in immediate cuts in steel and other related industries. The few promising signs of recovery in 1930 were dashed by business failures and layoffs.

The door was slammed shut on a quick recovery, and after 1930, business conditions in America declined across most sectors.

Although macro economic forces, international trade, stock and real estate overvaluation, and bad government policy started the Great Depression, it was the emotional element that caused it to last another decade.

You've heard it called the Depression Mentality. It is best described as a belief that the worst is yet to come. The manifestation of the Depression Mentality is a severe drop in investment, risk-taking, and spending. A weak and declining economy was driven deeper by a total lack of faith that it would get better anytime soon.

Modern-day Yale University economist Dr. Robert Shiller stated the driving force of the Great Depression very clearly in a lecture during the late 2000s:

"The problem at that time was very clear. Why were we in a Depression? It was that people perceived that we were in a Depression. It's as simple as that. If everybody thinks the whole economy is in a bad condition, it will be in a bad condition because everyone will pull back on all their expenditure plans. Entrepreneurs will decide, 'Well I'd like to be an entrepreneur, but not now.' So it all becomes a self-fulfilling prophesy."

What Dr. Shiller is describing is the consumer sentiment, or the emotional drivers of economic depressions. What is ironic is that Dr. Shiller has been one of the most outspoken pessimists in the media on the subject of the housing market. He has helped convince millions of people that this housing correction was a total meltdown. Given his awareness that irrational pessimism is a destructive force, I would have hoped he would be more careful with his public comments.

History records the bank failures that resulted from depositors losing faith in their bank and demanding, in unison, a return of their money.

What Ended the Great Depression?

Many historians believe that the Great Depression was ended by World War II, and the manufacturing, federal spending, and employment that it brought. After speaking with people who lived through it, I don't agree. The Depression was not just an economic phenomenon. It was an emotional one that was wired into the minds of too many Americans. This was not a crisis that could be solved by positive macro economic forces alone. It required an emotional boost to turn the Depression around.

It wasn't fighting World War II that ended the Great Depression. It was winning.

• • • • •

I am sure you can clearly see the similarities of the Great Depression to the Great Recession. Human nature is what it is, and it didn't change in the past 75 years.

The Great Depression was a unique historical event because of how long it lasted, more than how dramatically it began. The depth of the belief that the next shoe was about to drop made it impossible for any optimistic news to spark a recovery. It's like trying to start a fire with wet wood. It doesn't matter how hot the flame is. It won't ignite.

2 | SUCCESS STORIES FROM THE GREAT DEPRESSION

Time is running out to get firsthand accounts of the Great Depression from people who lived through it. People who were born in 1929 are in their 80s now. If they were old enough to remember the Depression, they are turning 90, at the youngest. These folks are the core of a generation that brought this nation out of an economic pit, won a world war, and gave us an America that was much more prosperous, safe, and fair than the one they inherited. The America they passed on to following generations was so good that some people believe that our generation is so spoiled that we are ruining it for the next.

It was enormously humbling and a ton of fun to sit and talk with people who lived through the Depression. They've seen how history has recorded the world events of their lifetime, and were eager to answer a different question: how did *your* family get by?

The goal here is to inspire you to see the glass as mostly full, and to take action to get your piece of the dream, recession be damned. I decided to tell the stories of people who did that in 1932, when things were a *whole lot worse* than they are now. What tools did Depression entrepreneurs have at their disposal to access opportunity? What kind of vision was needed to find opportunity when so little was evident? So many people were too afraid to spend their money, but what products did they still want and need? What was still in demand in America, despite the Depression?

The Pribish Family

John and Anna Pribish were Czechoslovakian immigrants that came to America at the turn of the century for opportunity, as everybody did back then. John and Anna had five kids, and in the mid 1920s, moved to Poughkeepsie, New York. I am married to their granddaughter, Leah Pribish, and this is the story of her family, as told to me by her Uncle Vinny. Vinny, who turned 90 in 2010, is the younger brother of Leah's Dad, John Pribish, who passed away in 1988.

The Pribishes bought a small two-story house in downtown Poughkeepsie. In order to make the most efficient use of their space and create a way to earn money, they moved the entire family up to the second floor, and gutted the first floor to build a grocery store. The whole family pitched in, but the driving entrepreneurial force in the family was Anna. Mamma was a bootstrapper.

The whole family also worked in the grocery store. When the stock market crashed a couple years later, and the Depression really began to set in, they had already moved to another property in uptown Poughkeepsie, where they did the exact same thing: gutted the first floor, moved the family upstairs, and built a larger store downstairs.

What was amazing about this story was how ingenious they were. They made the investment to increase the size of the store, thereby increasing the potential of their opportunity. Plus, they were thrilled to be in the food business because the number-one fear during the Great Depression was the inability to feed the family. They operated under the theory that, "If we own a grocery store, we'll always have food." Simple, yet brilliant.

However, it should not be taken for granted that food was easy to get. Retailers could not be guaranteed that they would always be able to find sources of food at wholesale prices for their store. It wasn't enough to just build the store. They had to find a way to stock it.

One day, a little red wagon showed up at the house, and the kids were all excited because they thought they had gotten a new toy. The parents put and end to that myth right away. This wagon was to be pulled by the children to the "Atlantic Pacific store" (you know it as A&P today) down the road to procure a 50-pound bag of sugar, and bring it home. The kids would take turns pulling the wagon both ways and when they came home, they were taught a business lesson they would never forget. They were shown how to break that big bag of sugar down into one-pound bags, put a price tag on them, and put them on the shelf. The kids were taught the concept of retailing, of buying products at wholesale, and then repackaging it to sell for a profit. They were taught another and more important lesson as well. There is money to be made on a bag of sugar if you put your brain and back into it.

Uncle Vinny explained that not long after, the kids watched as their mom took that wagon to the farmers' market and bought young chickens, turkeys, and "funny looking things called guinea hens." She would bring the chicks home and raise them in the backyard where the family built a chicken coop. Of course, they'd also stock up on turkeys in the fall so they could fatten them up in time for Thanksgiving.

Prohibition started in 1920 and lasted until 1933. The Pribishes had done well providing food, a product that was in great demand. Because the statute of limitations on bootlegging in the 1930s has expired, I will tell you how they diversified their product line. "After my mother did the laundry, which was on the stove in a big pot, she would use the pot to make beer." He later confirmed that she was a very clean woman and certainly cleaned the pot between uses. Not only don't people want beer that tastes like underwear, but they don't want underwear that smells like beer.

The Pribishes had three key natural resources at their disposal. First, the seven members of the family was a workforce of motivated people. Second, they had Mamma's entrepreneurial genius and drive. And finally, they had their real estate.

Real estate was at the center of their success. They didn't have the Internet back then. They didn't have the ability to create a widget and sell it online. They didn't have the ability to use social media to create a blog and sell advertising on it. The vehicle of their success was their real estate. They couldn't have a store unless they had a first floor to convert to a store. Without the backyard, there would be no henhouse. They weren't going to sell booze in the basement unless they had a basement. The raw material they had to work with was a combination of their own creativity, hard work, and their real estate.

The story takes an interesting turn as the Depression dragged on. The grocery store was a success. The family had food and a profitable business they could all pitch in to help run. Never satisfied with being idle, Anna found new opportunities and positioned the family to capture them.

Uncle Vinny recalled that one day a taxi showed up at the house, and the children were asked to help load the boxes of food they had just packed into the trunk. When they were finished, it drove off. The kids didn't ask questions, such as, "Where is that cab going?" They just did as they were told. (I wonder what that's like.)

Every week or so, the taxi would show up, they would load it up and off it would go. Until one day, a car showed up—*their* car! It was one of the only privately owned automobiles in their neighborhood. Uncle Vinny remembered making the connection between the appearance of the wagon, and then the car, and realizing that something was happening in their family. Something was going right. They were able to purchase an automobile, and now they were filling up their own car with this food and having it transported somewhere. The kids still didn't know where the food was going. All they knew was that there was a lot of food being packed up and sent off.

They later learned that the government had built a facility in the center of town to provide basic sustenance for people in need of a meal and a place to sleep. It was known as the Poor House. When the Poor House opened in Poughkeepsie, Anna and John filed the paperwork with the city and applied to become suppliers of food. To use contemporary business terminology, the Pribishes landed the biggest account in town.

Selling food to the Poor House enabled them to buy an automobile, which was a coveted possession at the time. That automobile was put to use for the family business, thereby justifying its purchase. Landing the Poor House account also enabled them to buy more real estate, and they bought property nearby and rented it out.

I have had the privilege of getting to know the children and grandchildren of John and Anna Pribish. I can see how the entrepreneurial education Uncle Vinny received as a kid shaped his world view. He has since been everything from a rocket scientist (seriously), to a banana farmer and importer, to a university professor, to a home builder, to the inventor of a revolutionary device that may just change the world as we know it. His life has been a beautiful series of can-do's. Not everything worked, but the creative drive was only made stronger by every experience. All of the Pribish grandchildren are the same way—no slouches in that group. They all pursued different paths and have become great successes. They share the optimistic outlook of their dads and grandparents.

The lesson here is simple, and it's one you know already. There is always opportunity. It's not always easy to seize, but it isn't supposed to be too easy.

The Reynolds and Parker Families

Allene Reynolds was celebrating her 95th birthday at the time of our interview, which means she was a teenager during the Depression. When I asked her about her experience during her childhood, she smiled and hesitated a bit. "I had a pretty good time. It wasn't so bad." I read her brief hesitation as the feeling that she is not supposed to admit what she was about to admit. I shared with her the premise of this book at the beginning of the conversation, so she knew it was safe to be honest.

Allene's experiece obviously doesn't jibe with the way history has recorded the Great Depression, so I knew I was in the right place. Allene wasn't being callous. She simply had a great childhood during the 1930s.

Her story was so intriguing to me because it involves two entrepreneurial corporations that had an enormous influence on Allene's life, her upbringing, and her family's ability to be depression-proof. And they were depression-proof in two senses; economically, because her father was able to make a good living, and emotionally. They were not depressed, despite the fact that the economy and the country were.

Allene's story begins in Janesville, Wisconsin, where her father was a manager for a cheese company. Kraft Foods, which had gone public in 1924, began a "roll up" strategy of buying food and dairy companies across the country. Kraft acquired the company Allene's dad worked for, and the whole family embarked on an adventure. They became mobile corporate nomads. Kraft Foods was expanding rapidly and Allene's dad was an executive on the transition team for those acquisitions. He would be transferred every few years to a new place to help assimilate a new acquisition into the Kraft Foods family of companies.

People used to say to Allene, "Aren't you sad you have to leave your school and your friends?" Her response was beautiful. "No, I'm going to make new friends. I can't wait to go to my new school."

In 1928, Kraft bought a cream cheese company in Philadelphia. Maybe you've heard of it. As always, the family packed up and moved to Philadelphia. A few years later, Kraft bought a mayonnaise company and they were off to New Jersey. Kraft then found Velveeta Cheese in Orange County, New York, and that's where Allene lives to this day.

Corporations are so often castigated for being evil, profit-seeking monsters, but as is so often case, this corporation's courage and ingenuity allowed it to continue to drive a growth strategy right through the Great Depression. Many families, including Allene's, were able to benefit from and contribute to that courage and ingenuity.

Kraft's growth wasn't all acquisition growth, either. Sales jumped in 1933 when Kraft introduced Miracle Whip. The company's sales then exploded with the introduction of a new product in 1937, in the heart of the Depression. The product was Kraft Macaroni and Cheese Dinner. What has since become a quintessential American side dish began as a low-cost way to feed the whole family. Kraft had a plan and a culture of optimism, and Allene's whole family was part of the team.

Allene's life was also touched by another entrepreneurial success story. Her uncle, George Parker, was the founder of the Parker Pen Company, which is still in operation today. He was an older man when the Great Depression began and he actually died during it. Allene's family did not share in the financial wealth of the Parker Pen Company, but they shared in something much more valuable—George Parker's example.

George Parker had been a salesperson for a pen company in the late 1800s. He then went on his own to start The Parker Pen Company and demonstrated to the entire family that someone who is enterprising can make his own way in America. Parker invented something called Quink in 1931, during the first part of the Great Depression. It was a quick-drying ink that made blotting ink unnecessary and was a major development in the pen industry. The company sold more than $400 million worth of pens worldwide and Parker Pens were the most widely used model of fountain pen in history.

During this period, Parker pens were used to mark some of the most momentous world events of the day, such as when General Douglas McArthur signed the document that officially ended World War II.

Allene and her grandson Ian Pinkney talked about Uncle George with admiration. He was a patriarch of the extended family. He taught the future generations of his family that success is possible. It doesn't need to be more complicated than that.

Through her upbringing, Allene did not look around and see only pain, suffering and hopelessness. She saw examples of inspiration, hope, and the entrepreneurial spirit. I think Allene summed it best when she said, "I had a pretty good time. It wasn't so bad."

The Harrington Family

I met Jack Harrington at a public hearing in my town where the city officials were discussing the possibility of acquiring a country club that was going under and turning it into a semi-private course. I sit in on municipal meetings all the time. That's how I get a sneak preview of what is coming soon to the markets that I am invested in. When the public had their chance to speak, most everyone agreed that they wanted the country club to remain green space, but there were several competing factions who saw different uses for the space. Should it become a semi-private course where members pay a low annual membership fee and then pay as they play golf, use the gym, and eat at the restaurant? Should it be a purely municipal facility, owned and operated by the Parks Department and turn the pool into a mini water park? And, as is always the case, there were environmental groups who wanted to turn the course into walking trails. (When someone can show me people who will pay $150 to walk on a trail, I will abandon the golf course approach and throw my support behind that business model.)

Near the end of the meeting, Mr. Harrington stepped up. He was a little slow moving, but with purpose and momentum, he stepped up to the podium. That's when he turned around to the people in the audience and said, "I've been around for a long time, and opportunities like this only come along once in a lifetime. I remember when there was green space all over this city, and now we have this condo project, this neighborhood of luxury houses, and this shopping center. Every time people start to squabble about nitpicky things like this, the opportunity slips away and the land gets bought by a private developer, and we all miss the chance to save the land."

Then he added, "And don't tell me about how this is bad timing. This recession is hard on a lot of people, but I lived through the real thing and this is not so bad."

Naturally, I chased him down after the meeting, introduced myself, and set up a breakfast interview. I wanted to hear more about the "real thing."

Jack was born in 1919 in Oswego, New York, which is on the banks of Lake Erie. He was 10 years old on Black Tuesday, and a rugged teenager through the entire Depression. His dad was a professional painter who had a stable, well-paying job, until he fell off scaffolding and broke half the bones in his body. Jack's mother had been a stay-at-home mom, but went to work out of necessity doing whatever she could to bring in the money they needed to survive. The family of seven scraped by.

Jack's dad barely had an elementary school education, and it made him fiercely committed to making sure his kids were as highly educated as possible. He and his wife were people of character. They had their beliefs about how a family should be raised and they stuck to their principals despite forces that might cause them to cut corners. Every Sunday, the family went to church. Every night, the family sat down for dinner. Every time they greeted another member of the community, it was "yes sir" and "yes ma'am." Every year, no matter how tight things got, Jack's dad would take him to the dentist. He believed it was important to keep one's teeth in good condition.

What struck me about this is not that it is so terribly unusual to have this kind of structure in a family, but this was a family with a seriously injured father who was knocked out of the workforce at a time when the family desperately needed his financial support. In other interviews that I didn't include in this book, that kind of bad luck was enough to drive a family right out of their normal structure and routine, and right into a life of volatility, despair, and chaos. Jack and his siblings knew there was a depression going on. They knew things were tough all over, including in their household. And yet, when I asked him to describe his experience of the Great Depression in one sentence, he said "I had a pretty good life."

This reinforced for me that the most important thing these Great Depression successes have in common is their mental toughness. The parents, as leaders of the family, refused to let the Depression destroy the mental health and optimism of their kids. The Harringtons did it by sticking with their routines, never complaining, and pushing themselves to continue with their educations. After all, there was life after the Great Depression. That simple belief, that the future is bright and this too shall pass, kept the things that were out of their control at bay, and kept *them* in control of their lives.

Jack joined the Marines during World War II, got his degree from Cornell University when he came home, and had a long and successful career as a vice president of marketing for a series of large insurance companies.

My question to you is this: what example are you setting during this Great Recession? Are you falling in with the populist pessimism? I think maybe you are not, because you picked up this book. Besides the wealth you will create by showing courage at a time when so many other people around us are showing fear, you are setting an example for the people in your life who depend on you. If there are little ones in your world, you are in the position to give them the same gift that the Pribish, Reynolds, and Harrington families gave their children: the power to see past the storm, and the power to be optimistic and clear-headed, even when times are tough. These kids were unlucky enough to be born into the

Great Depression, but they were very lucky indeed to be born into families who understood that happiness is not determined by what happens around you, but by how you respond to it. If the pursuit of happiness is the highest priority in your life, you have your priorities straight.

3 | A Participant's Explanation of the Great Recession

W e have to pick a point in recent years where the origins of the Great Recession first germinated. My own firsthand account of this economic crisis begins in the late 1990s. The information revolution that gave us ridiculous increases in productivity in the 1980s morphed into the Internet revolution, and everything accelerated exponentially. We are all accustomed to hearing about blow-out success stories of the modern era and being reminded that they did not exist just five years ago (YouTube, Facebook). And it's not hard to recall companies who were blow-out successes in the early 2000s, but seem like dinosaurs now (Palm, AOL). We have all gotten used to the

24-hour cable news cycle, in which a car chase is broadcast live across the globe. The pace of life is simply moving faster.

I believe the late 1990s is where the Great Recession began because it was when the short-attention-span, get-rich-quick, I-would-gladly-pay-you-Tuesday-for-a-plasma-TV-today mentality really began for my generation. This was the first time as adults that we saw the potential to turn a dollar into five dollars in the stock market by buying companies we knew almost nothing about, and that had no profits or revenues. The tech stock bubble taught a lesson that was very harmful and dangerous, and set us up for a fall less than 10 years later.

An unprecedented number of people began to trade in the stock market in companies with enormous sex appeal. We had new tools to access the markets, new television channels dedicated to indulging our desire to be more than amateur traders. Stories of young people making thousands a day were all around us. As someone who never got into the stock market before, I was a holdout. But after a few years of everyone partying without me, I jumped in. I had impeccable timing. As soon as I jumped in, the bubble burst.

Losing money wasn't the damaging lesson of the tech stock bubble, though. It was how painless the whole episode was after just a year. Yes, billions evaporated overnight for companies and individuals alike. People lost their retirement accounts. It was a disaster, and then it was over and a strong economy continued. There was no spike in unemployment. People did not change their spending behavior. Why are we experiencing the Great Recession today instead of 10 years ago when the stock market bubble burst? I'll leave that to economists and historians. All I know is that we moved right past it and it didn't change much of anything.

The housing market crisis, which presents the greatest opportunity to build wealth in this economy today, began the day the tech stock bubble burst. It was crystal clear to me at the time that Wall Street's volatile behavior scared a lot of people out of the stock market and drove them to real estate. This was a safe place to invest your money that paid lifestyle dividends. Buy a bigger place, and the whole family is happy with you. A home is a solid asset. It isn't so emotional and it's more under your control. It was a flight away from volatility and dependence on others toward stability and control. The real estate boom of the roaring 2000s was underway.

The second factor that kicked off the housing boom was the September 11th terrorist attack. I was running a regional real estate company at the time in the suburbs of New York City with my brothers and mom. When the Twin Towers fell, we all feared the economy was going to fall with them. But the opposite happened. The nation pulled together. Americans were encouraged by our leaders to continue to live our lives, and the economy went forward with momentum after just a few months of paralysis.

The public reaction related to housing was similar to the reaction after the tech stock bubble, but for different reasons. September 11th drove people to a heightened need for security and time with family. People wanted to lock themselves behind their front doors and play with their kids in their backyards. The important things in life become clear after a tragedy. One of the ways this manifested itself was a turbocharged housing market. Homes and real estate investments were in the highest demand in modern history. Government was deregulating, cutting taxes, and encouraging people to spend, invest, and borrow. It worked for years, giving the nation an economic boom with blistering appreciation of the real estate market, the stock market, corporate profits, and consumer lifestyle. Everyone was making money, but just like the Great Depression, there was instability lurking just under the surface.

4 | THE ANATOMY OF A HOUSING MELTDOWN

The "Housing Meltdown" is a term that was coined in the American media in 2006 when the Roaring 2000s started turning into the Great Recession.

It has been widely reported that loose lending practices, Wall Street greed, irresponsible behavior among consumers, and government meddling provided the perfect storm for a market backlash. Here is how it all looked from street level.

A perfect storm occurs when multiple fronts slam together. The first front of this storm was a consumer feeding frenzy of home buying. Home buyers were out in force beginning in 2002. It became routine that a new property that hit the market would be sold in a week, often in a bidding war. The market, which does swing like a pendulum from being a buyer's market to a seller's market, was at an extreme level. Sellers were the kings and queens of the market. Buyers were becoming accustomed to losing bidding wars, which is a painful experience. Imagine you and your spouse have decided "this is the one" and you make an offer. By this time, you are in love with the house. You are envisioning your furniture in the living room, your pictures on the mantle, your kids in the backyard, and your family having Thanksgiving dinner in the dining room. Then you lose the bidding war.

Certain innovative techniques began to go into practice, such as the "letter." The letter was something real estate agents would encourage a prospective buyer to write in the hopes that they would make an emotional connection with King and Queen Seller. The letter would go something like this:

Your Royal Highness, (not really)

My husband and I are genuinely enchanted by your lovely home. We feel warmth and family goodness in every room, and can see that you have built such happy memories there that we can only hope to live up to...

You get the idea. This sounds like a joke, but it actually worked and it illustrates what I call the Breath Mint Index. Picture a scene where sellers sat on their thrones and buyers bent and scraped at their feet trying to buy the palace, after being told by their real estate agent to comb their hair, leave junior in the car if he's being a brat, stand up straight, and take a breath mint. If real estate agents are recommending a breath mint to their buyers on the way into the house, this is a serious seller's market. Buyers wanted it bad, and everyone knew it.

The second front in this perfect storm was government meddling. At the highest levels in the federal government was a desire to lower the barrier of home ownership for more Americans. In principal, I agree with this mission. Homeownership is a great thing when it works out right, and it almost always does if you stick with the fundamentals (buy a house you can afford and stay there for a long time). Unfortunately, policy makers didn't understand the fundamentals.

The government controls Fannie Mae and Freddie Mac, often called the GSEs (government-sponsored entities). Think of the GSEs as the central bank behind the majority of home mortgages. Commercial banks and mortgage companies rarely lend to homebuyers out of their vaults anymore. They mainly lend GSE money. When the government sponsored the GSEs, they gave them preferential treatment that enabled them to lend money at lower rates than the private sector. Because everyone wants a low rate, the GSEs dominate the market they want to dominate, which is condos and one- to four-family houses. Mortgage companies and banks are essentially the front line retail sales arm of the GSEs.

The lending policy for the GSEs is the lending policy for the mortgage industry. The GSEs decide what it takes to qualify for a mortgage, and their masters in Washington were on a mission. They wanted money to flow.

The third front in the perfect housing storm was Wall Street. The housing market was hot and everybody wanted a piece of it. But Wall Street doesn't play by anyone else's rules, so they don't want to actually buy real estate and own it. They want to trade real estate, as fast and furiously as they can. In cooperation with the GSEs, they invented new instruments you have heard a lot about in the news: those mortgage-backed-securities-credit-swap-derivatives. Let's just call them poker chips.

Traders created a new marketplace to trade housing with poker chips, and the billions flowed. Demand for housing poker chips was just as hot for the demand for housing itself. In order to make it a really juicy market, Wall Street continued to add elements that encouraged volatility. The faster and more furious the trading, the more money to be made.

Buyers wanted mortgages and traders wanted more poker chips, but there was a problem. Not enough people qualified!

This brings us to the fourth and final front in the perfect real estate storm: lender amnesia. Back when our mortgage banking industry wanted loans to be paid back, they relied on three pillars of stability to approve a mortgage.

1. Skin in the game. Buyers were required put their hard-earned money down on the property. History showed that the more they put down of their money, the more likely they were to eat tuna out of the can for dinner and pay their mortgage if things got tight.

2. Good credit: You had to pay your bills on time. It sounds pretty obvious, but there is more to this than meets the eye. In the 1990s and prior, when banks made better loans, they relied on a credit profile, which included the actual credit report showing all the accounts a consumer has ever had, and how many times they paid late. This was the raw data, and it left room for interpretation by human beings called underwriters. A certain number and type of late payment was acceptable in certain circumstances. There was some subjectivity, and a lot of expense, so the industry invented the credit score, or FICO score. The concept was brilliant: boil a consumer's credit history down to one number. Either your score was above the threshold required and you got the loan, or it wasn't and you didn't. The mortgage lending industry took the human element out of the underwriting process and relied on the credit scoring system completely.

3. A job. How much do you make and can you prove it? Lenders knew, from decades of historical loan performance, that there is a percentage of gross income that a person can afford to pay for their housing payment, and that number was 28 percent. They also knew that there was a percentage that they could afford in other debts, which was another 8 percent. People who had a stable income and kept their payment below those thresholds would be fine. Lenders, including the GSEs, forgot or ignored these realities, and systematically increased the percentages borrowers were allowed to spend on their mortgage and other debt.

The four storm fronts; consumer frenzy, government meddling, Wall Street madness, and lender amnesia slammed together. This drove the GSEs and lenders to lower the down payment requirements down to zero. They lowered the credit scores down to where almost everyone qualified. And they invented the "stated income mortgage," which eliminated the requirement for a borrower to prove how much they earn.

The market responded as expected. Everyone got what they wanted. Buyers bought more and bigger homes. Government was achieving their utopia. Money was flowing like a raging river, but lurking just under the surface were two ticking time bombs.

The marketplace invented by Wall Street to trade their housing poker chips was built on quicksand. Despite the fact that every intelligent finance professional knows that markets are cyclical, the designers of the housing poker chip marketplace didn't build that into their model. In 2006, the cycle did what cycles do, and prices started coming down. Home prices had gone up dramatically during a six-year period, they peaked, and then began to correct, just as they had in the last five cycles. After sustained appreciation, the pendulum swings and some of the appreciation is given back.

The moment housing prices began to correct, Wall Street began their latest stampede. This time it was away from housing poker chips. Nationally, the value of housing had gone down less than 10 percent at that time, but the value of housing poker chips went down to almost nothing overnight. Mortgage-backed securities lost 95 percent of their value in a flash.

You know the result. The American Banking Industry, which had invested hundreds of billions of dollars in housing poker chips, saw their foundations crack before their eyes. Balance sheets of some of the most well-heeled, long-term players on Wall Street collapsed, not because of a housing meltdown, but because of a housing poker chip meltdown.

The next shoe to drop was the realization that a very high percentage of the loans that were made and then securitized were not going to perform and be repaid. The cascading effect culminated in October 2008 with a decline in home values that was totally predictable, yet blindsided the economy. Some banks failed and many more were likely to fail unless the federal government stepped in, and step in they did, with an unprecedented bailout of the banking and finance industry. What's more, in order to make sure everyone in America knew this was necessary, public officials from all branches of government raced to the microphone and shouted "the economy is going off a cliff!" and "This is the second Great Depression!" Without realizing it, or caring, they set the emotional side of a deep and long-lasting recession in motion. By scaring the public with superlatives about how horrible this economy was, they created a self-fulfilling prophesy. They convinced us that this was, in fact, the greatest economic disaster since the Great Depression, and so it became just that.

5 | WHERE ARE WE NOW?

Now we have irrational pessimism.

IRRATIONAL ¹ir·ra·tio·nal—*not endowed with reason or understanding (2): lacking usual or normal mental clarity or coherence*

In the 1930s, this country entered the emotional state of irrational pessimism, and yet millions prospered at the same time. Maybe the most famous success story from the

Great Depression was Joseph P. Kennedy, father of John F., Robert, and Teddy. He was a notorious businessman whose profiteering was the basis of a legend that made many view him as a business scoundrel. Some of that reputation was well-earned, because Kennedy did invent new ways to speculate in the stock market and bilk amateur investors. But Kennedy's wealth was built more by his business savvy and impeccable timing than by ripping other people off.

In the 1920s, Kennedy got into the movie business as that industry reached new levels of penetration into Everytown, U.S.A. Then he sold his interests just as that industry was about to consolidate. He was a very active stock market speculator who saw the writing on the wall when his shoe shine boy started giving him stock tips, and sold most of his positions just before the crash of 1929, when he began to sell the market short and capitalize on the misery of that historic event. It didn't make him popular, but it did make him rich. He then saw that Prohibition was likely to be repealed and set up lucrative contracts to import booze into the great American market that was about to be reopened.

All of these business successes made Kennedy a player, but it was his real estate investment timing that took the family fortune past the $100 million mark. Kennedy saw the American real estate market as the greatest place to park his assets during the Depression, and because he was one of the few buyers in that extreme seller's market, he made a killing. To this day, acquisitions he made during the Depression and World War II remain in his family.

Real estate investors at all levels, from the Pribishes to the Kennedys, were not afflicted by pessimism. The Pribishes used their real estate as the platform upon which to build a family business. The Kennedys used it as a place to park their assets once the Great Depression began. Both found incredible bargains because they were prepared to act when others were gripped by irrational pessimism. Both timed their investments at the beginning of a steady seven-decade run up in real estate values. In the real estate market, The Great Depression was The Great Overcorrection. Due to the state of the economy and the state of mind of the people, property sales plummeted and prices went lower than they should have.

Welcome to the second Great Overcorrection.

The Other Foreclosure Shoe Is About to Drop

To fully understand this you must get the timeline.

2000-2005: The housing market was booming. Prices were increasing 10 percent per year nationwide. Double that in hot spots such as Los Angeles, Las Vegas, Phoenix, Miami, and New York City. By 2005, we were already seeing a change in buyer attitudes. They were getting fed up with the ever-escalating prices and the attitudes of King and Queen Seller. We first noticed it at the beginning of 2005 when the bidding wars slowed down. Literally, talk in the industry was, "I can't believe this. I put 135 Maple Ave. on the market a week ago and no offers!"

2005-2007: By January 2007, prices began to decline in the hot spots and mortgage defaults began to go up. People with mortgages they couldn't afford were falling behind, and the slightest reduction in value was causing people to wonder why they should pay. Foreclosure alarms started going off in banks, government, Wall Street, and the media even though much of the nation was not affected yet. All hell broke loose in October 2008, and the credit crisis wrought havoc. The response from many prominent politicians was to dive in front of any camera they could find and say things such as:

- "Banks acted in a predatory manner and must be held accountable."

- "Borrowers were lured by lenders to take loans they can't afford."

- "Borrowers who were victimized must be given relief and help from the government."

This push by the government took place at the same time that the government was making the decisions of who got bailed out (AIG and Citibank), who got bought out (Merrill Lynch and Countrywide) and who was allowed to hit the wall (Bear Stearns and Lehman Brothers).

The government put pressure on banks to put a moratorium on foreclosures. That moratorium was followed by measures designed to prevent foreclosures, such as loan modification and debt forgiveness programs. All the while, the economy got worse, and none of those solutions alleviated the pressure in the foreclosure pipeline. A log jam of defaulting mortgages began piling up as the borrowers stopped making payments and lenders held off on foreclosing.

At the same time, banks had incentives not to foreclosure on defaulting borrowers. Their motivation is always to sure up their stock price by making their balance sheets look as good as the law will allow. Balance sheets are a measure of a company's assets. Mortgages that are in default are classified differently on a balance sheet than mortgages that are closed out by a foreclosure action where the bank repossesses the property. Banks have to realize certain losses when they foreclose, and absorb the hit, which is made much worse if the market is declining. How do you put a value on a house that is losing value? This presents a major incentive for banks to hold off and kick the can down the road a bit. What were they waiting for? Real estate values to hit bottom. That is happening at the time of this writing, and the banks are beginning the massive task of repossessing millions of properties.

What's more, new trends of creative mortgages took shape a few years ago. What makes an exotic loan exotic is that you only pay interest, and don't pay the mortgage balance down over time. The build up of equity and wealth would only take place when the property appreciates, or when the borrower showed the discipline to send in more than their required payment. A particularly egregious version of these loans were known as "payment option" loans, where borrowers had the ability to make a payment that was *less* than the minimum interest owed. It was their option to tack on more debt to their existing balance. Sounds like a credit card, right?

You may have heard about the adjustable rate mortgages "resetting" in the coming years. Those stories refer to the fact that exotic mortgages are a ticking time bomb. The borrower's right to pay only the interest, or minimum payment, is temporary. When the bank withdraws that option, their payment shoots up, making many borrowers unable to pay. This is a second wave of loan defaults that will be coming our way.

Millions of bank-owned properties will be brought to market at a time when irrational pessimism lingers. In fact, the foreclosure wave itself will be fuel for that pessimism. You might be thinking that this sounds like a horrible economic forecast. It isn't. A few million properties being brought to market in the next few years will be absorbed by the market, just as they were in places such as California and Florida before the foreclosure moratoriums began. Some people hear this and disagree. They will quote platitudes about the worst economic crisis since…

Are they willing to predict that Apple will not be able to sell the next iPhones, vacationers will have no waits at the rides at Disney, and there will be no such thing as the hottest restaurant in town?

They would not make those predictions. Fun, food, and toys never go out of style. Neither does living indoors. This is the Great Real Estate Over-Correction of our generation.

6 | You Can Own America

In the following pages, I will prove to you that American housing is the best asset you can invest in. It is the best business you could ever be in. It is the best stock you could ever own.

Reason #1: It's America

The United States of America is the most prosperous, free, liberated nation in the history of the planet. What was started as an act of rebellion against oppressors became the most brilliantly designed platform ever conceived to align a nation's governing principles with the best in human nature.

Within the preamble of the Declaration of Independence are words that I believe are the most important words ever written. That we are endowed with the rights to "life, liberty and the pursuit of happiness." It is the pursuit of happiness that established a direct connection with the very best aspects of human nature: optimism; wanting to be more than you are; the right to work as hard as you want to achieve happiness, as defined by you.

This is the beacon of hope that has caused generation after generation of immigrants from every country in the world to come here. They, as human beings, are wired to desire happiness, and this is the country that was set up to help allow them to pursue it.

The most innovative, creative, and ingenious inventions of the last two centuries were invented here, from the light bulb to the assembly line, from the automobile to the airplane, from the television to the video game, from the personal computer to the Internet—all made in America.

You get it, so how incredible is it that you can own a piece of it? Not just a place in which you can live, but an asset class in which you can invest, or create a business with which you can create incredible wealth. America is for sale, right now. In fact, it's *on* sale.

When the U.S. Constitution was adopted in 1787, it was deemed to be missing some specific language that caused some concern among the representatives of the states that the federal government could become too powerful. The representatives felt there was a need to amend the Constitution, and they wrote the first 10 amendments, which were known as the Bill of Rights. In the preamble of the Bill of Rights, it was stated that several delegations from the states, "having at the time of their adopting the Constitution, expressed a desire, in order to prevent misconstruction or abuse of its powers, that further declaratory and restrictive clauses should be added." In other words, the Constitution states how the nation would be governed, and the relationships among the branches of the federal government and with the state governments. The anxiety that was expressed at the Constitutional Convention by many of the delegations was that it did not state clearly what protections the people had from intrusion by the government. Hence, the Bill of Rights was created.

Ownership of America by Americans was prescribed and referenced several times in the Bill of Rights, but the Fifth Amendment is where property rights are guaranteed. It stated that individuals could not be "deprived of life, liberty, or property, without due process of law; nor shall private property be taken for public use, without just compensation." In other words, when you own real estate in America, you own it. Intruders can not enter. Even the police can't enter without due cause, and your real estate can not be taken away without due process *and* just compensation.

When you own real estate in The United States of America, the value of your asset is supported by all that makes the country strong, prosperous, safe, and in-demand.

Reason #2: It's Housing

Did living in hollowed-out trees come back into style when I wasn't paying attention? Are moms and dads everywhere excited about their grown children moving back home for the rest of their lives? Do families of four enjoy sharing a one bedroom apartment all of a sudden? No! All newborn babies need a roof over their heads.

Politicians fight on a daily basis about who has the better solution to our "immigration crisis" as they call it. Think about the nature of that crisis. People from around the world will do anything to live here. They will leave their families, risk their lives, and break the law to get here if they have to. Some cynical Americans will respond by saying that our country is not as good as it used to be. Maybe, maybe not, but it's still better than anywhere else, and the population trends prove that.

Population in the United States doubled in the last 100 years. It is projected that it will increase another 40 percent by 2050. The main driver of housing demand is very simple. More people equals more demand.

Two-thirds of the United States population own their home, leaving one-third as renters.

Homeownership in the United States reached its peak in 2004 at 69.2 percent. People are wired to want to own their own home, and when government and lenders enable more people to do it, they will. Now those trends have reversed themselves and homeownership is slowly declining, dropping to 66.9 percent in mid-2010. That represents more than 6 million people who went from being owners to being renters.

More than 800,000 rental households were created in 2009 alone, and the trend toward renting is going strong. Those are new tenants who are paying more than five billion dollars in *new* rent every year. Many people would agree that this is not a great time to be a business owner, or invested in the stock market, or even a homeowner. But it is a great time to be a landlord.

This economic crisis is not only providing investors with the opportunity to get a deeply corrected price, but it comes with a wave of new renters who need a place to live.

Another interesting trend of this new wave of renters is the type of rental they prefer. Even with the huge increase in rental households, vacancy in large apartment buildings is up, meaning there are more vacant apartments than previous years, despite the increased demand for rental units. Where are all these people moving to? They are renting single-family and two- to four-family houses.

It makes sense. People are going from homeowner to renter in large numbers. They may not be able to own a home, but they still want to live in one. It's the backyard factor.

So as you consider taking the plunge into real estate investing at this unique point in history, start your evaluation at the very highest level. What is it you are investing in? How powerful are the forces of demand for it? How likely are those forces to continue into the future? Is it likely that demand will decline for some unforeseen reason?

The answers to all of these fundamental questions are strongly in support of a robust and vibrant rental market well into the future, and an improving economy that will support property values in most parts of the country. The stars are aligned to make this the best time in modern history to be a landlord.

7 | PREDICTABILITY

I magine I am presenting myself to you as the finest me-
teorologist in the world. My track record is better than
any other weather man, living or dead. I have predict-
ed the weather accurately 100 percent of the time since I
made my very first prediction 20 years ago. You would be
impressed and you would want a demonstration of my uncanny abilities. Imagine we are in New York, it's January 1,
and you say "show me."

I power up my computer, pull out my charts, grab my
chin, and stare off into space for a moment or two as I con-
template the future, and what it will look and feel like. My

eyes come back into focus, and I state with authoritative confidence, "It will be approximately 20 degrees warmer in April, and 20-30 degrees warmer than that in July. Then it will start getting colder around September, and be back to freezing by next January."

You would have walked away by the time I got to January. There is nothing remarkable about predicting that a cycle will cycle. Everyone experiences the weather cycle. We fully understand what is coming next because we have experienced it so many times.

Some of us have experienced another cycle, one that relates to human behavior more than the laws of nature. Imagine you get an invitation in the mail to a wedding—in the Bahamas. It's a good enough friend that you can justify the expense and you start making plans. The location is a beach resort, and the Website shows an awesome pool with a swim-up bar, hot tubs, a gorgeous beach, blue water, and people playing volleyball. Then you picture yourself in those images and you don't fit in. Something is terribly wrong. You are not a model. You need to get in better shape for this occasion. And so the cycle begins.

A new motivation takes hold of you. Granola for breakfast, salad for lunch, and a sensible dinner. No peanut butter at 2 a.m.

You go to your gym for the first time since you joined. You even buy new workout clothes and cross-training shoes.

As the big day approaches, you are pleased with the results. You're still not a model, but you are a better-looking version of you than what would have shown up on that beach if you had not gotten your groove on.

The big day comes and you have a blast. You feel great about yourself because you took control and can now reap the benefits. So you celebrate, and celebrate…and celebrate. Before you know it, you've gained it all back.

The cycle is complete when you get back to being your old self. Every pound of the old you is back. No worse for wear. You have some great memories and some pictures you don't have to sneak into the trash can.

If you are one of those lucky people with a metabolism that takes care of this for you, or you have the sustained discipline to keep it going, congratulations. I believe you can still embrace the example.

Cycles are very predictable, whether they are driven by the laws of physical nature or human nature, and life is better when you can predict the future with some accuracy. Greg the weatherman wasn't a psychic, he just understood the cycle. Greg's wife does not need to be a psychic to predict he will get chubby again after the beach wedding is over. She just knows her man. She could predict a repeat of the cycle. Let me show you how to predict another cycle and take the risk out of one of the most important decisions of your life: where to invest your money.

Before we get into the cycle itself, we must establish the correct perspective. If you are trying to see down the road, first you need to stand up straight and improve your vantage point.

Vantage Point

When the computer revolution arrived in the mid-1980s, it impacted every business in different and interesting ways. Often, the introduction of lighting-fast computing was a game-changer. It enabled businesses to do things that were never possible before, and sometimes illuminated things that were never known before. Securities trading was such an industry. It wasn't that long ago that stocks were traded by a linkage of phones that led from the clients all the way to the stock exchange floor. The end user might have a tickertape, but not the real-time quotes and charts that the computer revolution made possible. Around the end of the 1980s, it became evident to investors that stock charts are not smooth lines running up, down, or sideways. When you look at them up close, you can see that they pulsate along the way. Split-second trading activity creates split-second fluctuations in price. In other words, even though stock in Ford Motor Company might be enjoying a nice steady upward trajectory, if you zoom all the way in, you see it is going *up-down-up-down-up-down* all the way.

This vibration is a reality; a micro-cycle that traders learned quickly how to use to make money. What was soon labeled as the "day trader" trend was essentially made up of investors who could use modern technology to trade on the micro-cycle and turn a dollar into two dollars with incredible consistency. In the subsequent years, hedge funds got into the game and proved that they could turn 10 million dollars into 20 million dollars just as consistently. The vibration is a reality.

The housing market is no different. It goes up and down in a predictable fashion that can be shown on a chart. But in order to see the housing cycle, you don't zoom all the way in, you *zoom all the way out.*

The housing cycle will typically last 12–15 years, and *what* takes place during those years can be counted on. *When* they take place is never known in advance, so the trick is to know what will come next, and what are the first signs that it's approaching. Those outward signs will fall into three categories: economics, demographics, and attitudes. All of these have an impact on demand for housing. Watch the demand (the buyers), and you can predict what is coming next.

The seven phases of the housing cycle are:

1. Stability: Everything is status quo.

2. Revival: The market begins to appreciate.

3. Boom: Appreciation curve steepens.

4. Peak: Appreciation stops.

5. Correction: Some appreciation is given back. Values come down.

6. Bottom: The opposite of the peak.

7. Stability: Cycle resets.

I will show you this cycle from several angles and you will internalize something that will change the way you grasp this asset class. This is probably the most important foundational element that makes professional investors successful. If you have faith in the cycle, you also have faith in the long-term appreciation of the asset. Real estate values have always ended the cycle higher than where they were when the cycle began.

Here is the housing market through three cycles. You will begin to see the patterns emerge when you observe how history repeats itself three times.

Cycle A: 1968–1982

The word that best describes the economy in the 1970s is stagnant. By the middle of the decade, the nation was in a recession that had already lasted two years. Home sales were low, but home prices continued to appreciate steadily. Some economists credit government intervention in the form of tax credits and a mortgage subsidy program, but I see it differently. Demographics, more than economics, drove prices up in the 1970s. Baby Boomers were having kids and buying homes despite the fact that the economy was lousy.

What began as a gradual curve upward in property values then steepened. As prices rose to a point that the market would no longer support, appreciation stopped when buyers refused to follow this curve any higher. By the end of the 1970s, the economy was in poor shape. High unemployment, high interest rates, high inflation, a gas shortage, and low consumer confidence punctuated the economic conditions. As a result of those factors and the fact that prices had sustained a long period of appreciation, prices peaked and corrected a bit. High interest rates that reached 17 percent were the most significant driver. People could afford the payment, but that payment bought less house when rates skyrocketed. Demand weakened until sellers lowered their prices. In this case, the market did not correct much, but simply leveled off. This is the natural progression of the market cycle:

- Cycle begins at a low point.

- Market appreciates as demand grows.

- Market cools off because prices rise too high, and the economic climate worsens.

United States Housing Market
Single-Family Median Price

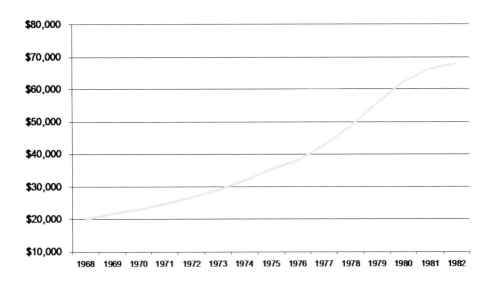

- Market corrects when sales slow down and sellers eventually capitulate.

- Market levels off as demand comes up to meet the new price levels. Market remains level until the economy accelerates again.

- Cycle is complete.

The goal is not to know exactly when the next segment of the cycle will come, but to know what it will look like when it arrives. When mortgage rates climbed higher than 12 percent in 1980 as a result of federal policy to fight inflation, it was predictable that demand would fall off. It did, and the cycle moved on to the next phase.

Cycle B: 1983–1996

In the early 1980s, the economy was still in rough shape. High inflation, interest rates and unemployment were dragging the overall economy down and keeping home values flat. Those years were followed by the economic boom of the 1980s (commonly referred to as the Decade of Greed). Leveraged buyouts in the corporate world, enormous growth in commercial real estate development, tax cuts, and the invention of the personal computer gave us a period of economic growth in all sectors of the economy. Home values rose, and the curve remained steady.

United States Housing Market
Single-Family Median Price

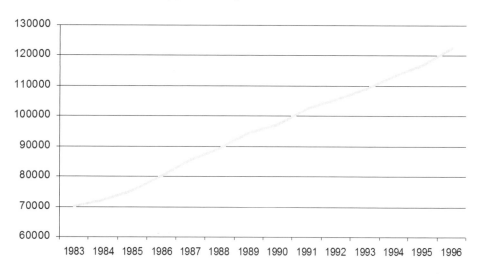

Along the way, the stock market got overheated and overvalued, and crashed in 1987, and speculative development and lending practices necessitated an unprecedented bailout of the nations banking industry. Sounds familiar, I know. Many people recall that the real estate market made an ugly correction at the end of the 1980s, but that does not apply to the national market. The hottest real estate markets, such as New York and California, saw steeper appreciation first and then a correction at the end. Nationally, however, it was a steady climb.

The predictor for the end of this cycle was the stock market crash and bank bailout that occurred after a sustained period of appreciation. The economy was basically overheated, but as you will see in the next cycle, stock market busts don't necessarily create havoc for the housing market.

Cycle C: 1997–20??

Interestingly, the 1990s were good economic times, fueled by the second wave of the Information Age: the Internet. Most of the economic benefit came from increased productivity and exuberance in the stock market, specifically in dot-com companies. It was not an overall economic boom because the housing market was steady, but slow during the 1990s.

United States Housing Market
Single-Family Median Price

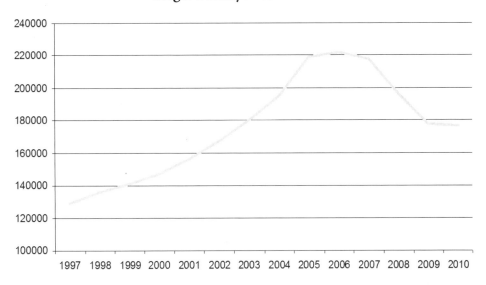

Then we entered a recession in 2000 after the tech stock bubble burst. You might expect that financial disaster to have a negative impact on housing, but housing was quiet for the entire preceding decade. Housing was due for a boom, and the tech stock bubble actually lit the fuse. As was discussed previously, the tech stock bubble was not just a correction in values on Wall Street. It was evidence of wild-eyed volatility on Wall Street. For years leading up to that event, online trading firms had been enabling millions of amateur investors to trade their own accounts. Why do you think so many companies with little revenues and no profits were able to have their stock prices driven up so high? Because the amateurs were evaluating stocks based on the sex appeal of their story, not on their price-earning ratio. And the professionals were encouraging them to do it.

The tech stock bubble drove investors away from Wall Street and right into the arms of the housing market, where great values and lifestyles could be found.

I've also described the impact of September 11th on the American attitude toward housing, which heightened the population's desire for homeownership.

By 2003, the economy was booming, this time led by the housing market. You can see the market rose steeply. Again, overdevelopment, loose lending practices, and buyer exuberance carried the market too far. The stock market crashed in late 2008 when the credit crisis hit, and the government needed to bail out the banking industry again.

At this time, I was ra partner in a large regional real estate, mortgage, and insurance company. I was up to my ears in this cycle, and this is where I learned to read the attitudes of buyers and sellers, and predict the market's movements based on what I saw.

During the boom, there was an incredible imbalance in the negotiating stature of buyers and sellers. King and Queen Seller looked down their noses at the buyers who would do anything to please them, just for the privilege of overpaying for their house. Back then, my purpose of predicting the market's next move was not for the sake of analyzing the market on TV or radio, but for the sake of expanding and growing the company. We timed our expansion perfectly, beginning in 1997, to acquire real estate brokerage offices and adding other allied companies to our portfolio. The pedal was pressed to the metal, and our founder and CEO, my mom and mentor, Marsha Rand, would always impart her wisdom to her sons with a wagging finger. She'd tell Joe, Matt, and me, "Don't expect this to last! These hot markets never do! I remember back in 1981…" This was Mom's third trip to the party, her third cycle. She knew that it would change. It was our job to watch closely for signs that it was happening and put the brakes on our expansion.

We saw it coming in early 2005 when the bidding wars slowed down. Something was up with buyers. They were tired of paying ever-escalating prices to sellers who were treating them like dogs. They got fed up, and the first place it showed was at the point of negotiation. Buyers got frustrated, then they got cautious. Eventually they got downright cocky. We saw this change as a very early indicator that the market was beginning to shift and put the brakes on our expansion. We had been adding two new real estate brokerage offices to our company every year for seven years straight through either acquiring an existing company or opening from scratch. We were pouring money into our expansion and needed to know when the market was going to shift because it could be a crippling mistake to incur those kinds of costs when the market slowed down.

It took three years before the market truly changed, as measured by the statistic you see reported in the news, but we nailed it with plenty of time to complete the deals that were in our pipeline, and then just sat tight.

As an aside, our next mission was to wait until the market was at its absolute worst, and slam the expansion pedal back to the floor, which we did in May 2009 with the biggest expansion announcements in our history. We bought competitors at the time when the market was at its worst, but we sensed it was about to start improving again. That intuition was based on the steepness of the correction. Our market dropped so quickly that we were back at 2003 prices again. Remember that it was 2005 when buyers began to get fed up, so we believed the price gains in 2006 and 2007 were momentum-driven. We believed the market would drop back to 2005 levels and then begin to recover. The fact that it fell straight to 2003 levels was, in our opinion, an overcorrection, and therefore time to attack. We did not anticipate this deep of a recession, and so prices appeared to be rolling back as far as 2001 levels, which is certainly an overcorrection.

What do I see next? As this market finds its bottom, which is what is occurring at the time of this writing, it will flatten out and stay there for five years. This cycle was very similar to the previous cycle. After the hot burn of the 1980s, things froze. It took most of the 1990s and an economic boom to fully thaw out, but the revival came. It's coming again.

8 | THE SUPPLY AND DEMAND PENDULUM

As you visualize the housing market cycle, you will observe that the pendulum swings from one side (seller's market) to the other (buyer's market).

At one extreme is a seller's market, which we had between 2002 and 2005. Sellers were in control. Buyers were desperate. Prices rose.

At the other extreme is a buyer's market, which we have now. Buyers are in control. Sellers are desperate. Prices are falling. The only homes selling are the ones where buyers are getting their price.

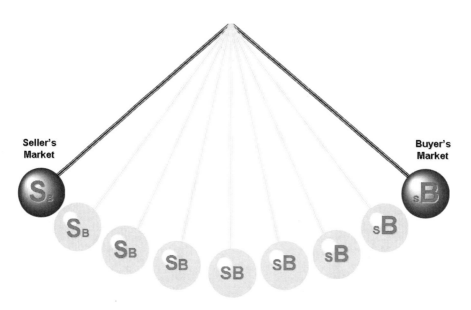

The pendulum is representative of the negotiating posture of buyers and sellers. The places in the market cycle curve where the market changes are and where the pendulum begins to swing. When the market cycle curve goes from flat to appreciation, buyers are eager, and sellers will begin to feel confident. As the appreciation continues, sellers will get cocky and buyers will get anxious and eventually fed up. When the market crests and prices stop appreciating, that is because the buyers became stubborn, sales stagnated, and sellers finally gave in and lowered their prices. When prices are falling, buyers are the ones who can get overconfident because sellers are at a clear disadvantage.

When the market finally finds a bottom, we find ourselves on a level playing field. Neither buyer nor seller has a distinct market advantage, and that situation won't change until the next economic boom drives prices up and the cycle begins again.

When the housing cycle chart is on its way up, it is time to think about selling. The ideal time to sell is just before it crests because the crest is when buyers begin to get squeamish and cautious. Some of the control sellers find in a seller's market disappears once the buyers show signs of stubbornness. You want the numbers on your side (increasing prices) and you also want the attitude on your side (buyers who are still hungry and not yet getting their confidence back).

The time to buy is when the values are just about bottoming out. Sellers are at their most vulnerable at that moment. Once the market bottoms, sellers lose that feeling of a "free fall" and get their confidence back. That translates into a stronger negotiating posture among sellers.

The closer you can get to understanding the attitudes of the people who represent supply (sellers) and demand (buyers), the better-equipped you will be to understand what comes next. Attitudes drive behavior. Behavior drives actions. Actions are represented in the actual buying and selling activity that shows up in the housing statistics months later. If you want to know which way real estate prices will go in six months, find out how buyers and sellers are feeling today.

So there is good news and better news. First, the market is finding a bottom and the cycle will get ready to reset all over again. Second, you are aware of it at a very early point, and, third, you have plenty of time to get your assets in gear and make an investment.

OwnAmerica.com is the accompaniment for this book that enables you to view the market cycle for any zip code in the United States. Researching the market you know best is probably the best place to start.

Ask yourself, was there a meltdown here? Did prices collapse? Of course not. Prices flattened out in most places at a level that is significantly higher than in the year 2000. There are some places in the country where the boom was so hot that the bust gave back all the appreciation. There are others that quietly and unremarkably appreciated during the boom, and have remained quite stable since.

This is proof that you can't believe the pundits who called this a housing free fall. This was a very profitable real estate cycle that made a lot of people a lot of money. Many investors got hurt in this cycle, but most of them ignored the fundaments and tried to buy and flip with no money down. That's the sucker's bet in real estate.

Work real estate into your long-term plan and you will already have two very strong advantages: a long-term view and a well-timed cycle.

9 | FUNDAMENTALS: THE DRIVERS OF REAL ESTATE WEALTH

If someone told me 10 years ago that 11 million people would have screwed up homeownership, I wouldn't have believed them. The housing crisis that ended the Roaring 2000s was the first time in history that so many people got bad results in real estate, and as we've been discussing, there were several variables that were introduced in this cycle that had not been present before. Exotic loans, bad lending practices, government hyper-promotion of homeownership, Wall Street mortgage mania, and wild consumer expectations, to name them.

Talk to 10 people who are financially comfortable and ask them how they did it. For most of them, real estate was a major factor, if not *the* factor.

When done right, real estate ownership is a universally proven and accepted way to get rich, but how does it work? People who buy real estate they can afford and hang on to it for a long time materialize wealth. Is it pure luck that created such great results for the vast majority of owners?

Of course not. There are technical drivers of real estate wealth that do not exist together in any other form of investment. The synergistic relationships between appreciation, leverage, amortization, and income generation are like a beautiful symphony. People know how well their stocks and mutual funds perform. It's right there on the statement. Real estate doesn't have a statement, and until now, it was too complicated to figure out. If real estate did have a statement, I think the stock market would lose half of its customers overnight. A stable, easy to manage piece of real estate quietly produces double digit returns that would embarrass most professional fund managers. Here is how it works.

Think of appreciation, leverage, amortization, and income as four dials on a mixing board in a sound studio. As you push each of them up a little bit, the volume gets exponentially louder. You don't need any of them to perform off the charts to get off-the-charts results.

U.S. Census Single-Family Home Prices Adjusted for Inflation

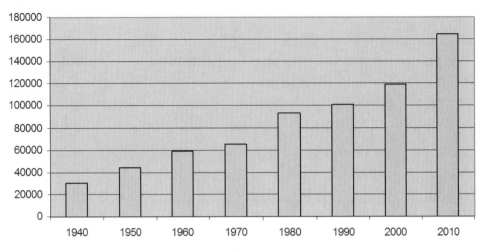

The First Dial: Appreciation

The American housing market has appreciated during every 10-year period in modern history.

In fact, home values in the United States did not nationally decline once since the Great Depression. Even after the "housing meltdown" we are experiencing today, home values have remained well above where they were 10 years earlier. If this doesn't jibe with what you have heard or read in recent years, that is probably because of the way certain economists and media outlets have used narrow samples to show extreme headline-getting results. According to the U.S. Census and the National Association of Realtors, the steady trajectory is still in tact.

The housing market does not want to appreciate at double-digit percentages. It wants to grow at 3–4 percent a year. If it gets too hot, it will correct, but demand for housing is tied to population, which is growing.

United States Housing Market Single-Family Median Price

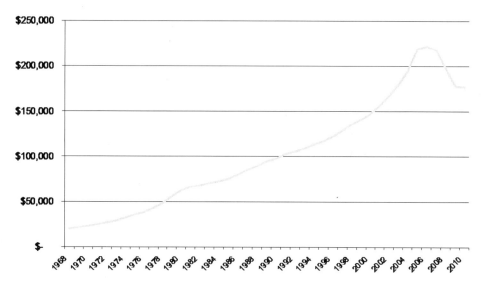

Many people will see the recent decline on values as a harbinger of the "new reality." That is nonsense. Home values went too high for some very specific reasons that have been taken out of the equation. Now the market is almost done correcting, and we may be back to 2001 home prices before we are finished. That means that the *entire bubble* has been erased. *Poof!* Gone.

Real estate will continue to appreciate now that the anomaly of the Roaring 2000s has been dealt with by the market. What will follow is a flat line of values for a period that should last five years, and then the market will begin to creep up again. Then, when we get our next economic boom, the revival of housing values will come.

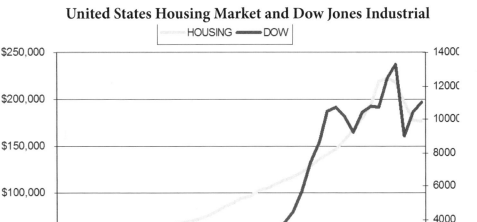

United States Housing Market and Dow Jones Industrial

The Second Dial: Leverage

When comparing real estate to other asset classes, the most common comparison is to the DOW Jones Industrial Average. Financial experts who do not understand real estate make a side-by-side comparison and don't realize they are comparing apples and oranges. The difference is leverage. The charts for U.S. Housing and the DOW are strikingly similar. Both have done very well in the past 40 years. The DOW was around 900 in 1968 and has grown to 11,000 by now. That's an increase in value of more than 1200 percent.

Nationally, the median price of a single family home in 1968 was $20,100, and has grown to $176,000. That's an increase of 880 percent, so the DOW performed better, right? Maybe technically, but this is where leverage comes in. Most people take out a mortgage to buy real estate, so the actual cash invested is much less when compared to the return.

If a buyer puts 25 percent down on a property, ($25,000 on a $100,000 house) and the property appreciates by 2.5 percent (making it worth $102,500), the investor has gotten a 10-percent return that year ($25,000 is now $27,500).

If an investor put $25,000 into the stock market in 1968, he would have about $300,000 at the time of this writing, a total appreciation of about 1200 percent. If that investor used that same $25,000 as a down payment on a property that cost $100,000, that property would have grown to be worth $880,000 in that time, and the mortgage would be paid off. That's a return of $860,000 on a $25,000 investment, or 3200 percent. Real estate blows away the stock market by a factor of almost triple.

Some experts and stock market defenders will quote things such as dividend reinvestment as a way the stock market would have added more value. That's a fair point, and in response I would point out how rental properties generate a profit, especially in all the years after the property was paid off. We will focus on cash flow right after we discuss real estate's third wealth driver.

The Third Dial: Amortization

The third driver of wealth creation in housing investment is amortizing, or paying down the mortgage. (Or more accurately, having tenants that pay down the mortgage.) The following table illustrates the amortization of a standard 30-year, fixed-rate mortgage. The longer the property is held, the faster the equity is built. This is another reason why it is critical to take a long-term view when investing in housing.

30-Year Mortgage Amortization

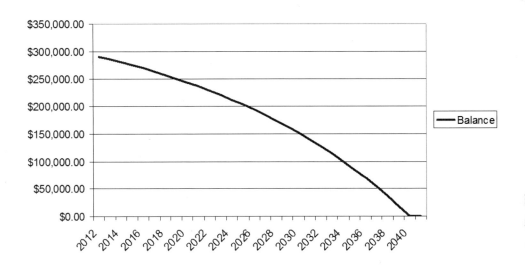

A 15-year, fixed-rate mortgage builds equity much faster on a much steeper curve.

15-Year Mortgage Amortization

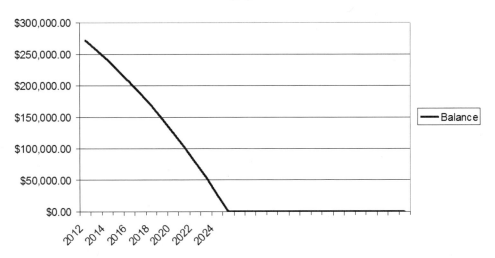

When history records the housing crisis of the 2000s it will have a special section on "exotic mortgages." You may have heard the term and wondered about the real nature of these bizarre instruments, and more importantly, their origin.

The first of the exotics was the interest-only loan, and the first time I ever heard of one was when my brother Matt told me about it. He had heard it from…wait for it…his stock broker. It was a piece of creative financing that was designed, according to Merrill Lynch, for "high net worth individuals" who "had a higher level of sophistication." The idea is that you would have a smaller mortgage payment for the same loan balance and pay down your principal on your own. You had total control over your mortgage, which meant most people didn't pay it down at all. What's more, they would flip it around so instead of getting the same mortgage and paying less in payments, borrowers used interest-only loans to make the same payment, but borrow more money. The market was saturated with interest-only loans, especially when the lending guidelines were relaxed. It was all about maxing out your borrowing power.

I viewed it as a way for Wall Street to get their hands on your home equity. The average account holder at a major bank has a balance of a few thousand dollars. The average mortgage balance at the same bank is in the hundreds of thousands. It's a juicy market Wall Street wanted to get their hands on, and they did.

On the scale of "exotic," where a 30-year, fixed-rate is like a trip to Disney World, and an interest-only loan is like a Caribbean vacation, the "option arm" would be like a weekend on the moon.

With an option arm, you had the option to totally screw up your real estate ownership experience. Here how this abomination worked. You could make the 30-year, fixed-rate payment, or you could make the interest-only payment, *or* you could take the option of making the minimum payment, which is just like a credit card minimum payment. In this case, your mortgage balance would actually go up instead of down. The first time I heard about these things was on a conference call with a major lender (I was running a mortgage company at the time). They introduced us to this equivalent of Frankenstein's Monster, and told us they were paying a premium to mortgage brokers to sell this loan. When I asked why it was considered more valuable than a normal mortgage, they replied, "It's beautiful. Borrowers pay more and more interest, forever!"

You might remember a particularly egregious TV commercial for a product like this. It showed a cute and modest little white house. The voice said "With other lenders' mortgage loans, you can afford *this* house, but with our option arm, you can afford *this house!*"

The camera panned right to reveal that the quaint little cape cod home was actually just the garage of a mansion. I am not a believer that lenders were universally predatory during the boom, and there is plenty of blame to go around, but that ad was a horror. It might not surprise you to learn that the same mortgage company who ran that ad jumped in with their "responsible lending" message as soon as the crisis hit.

We know how this all played out. As soon as the housing market ran out of steam and began to correct, everyone freaked out. Those lenders who were certain that homeowners would pay more and more interest forever watched in stunned disbelief as those borrowers began to default.

The lesson is simple. Don't tamper with the fundamentals. Buy property you can afford, make a sizeable down payment, and pay that sucker off during an extended period of time. Anything else is unnecessarily risky.

The Fourth Dial: Income

When the current rental income exceeds the expenses to own and operate the property, the result is positive cash flow. Every dollar of positive cash flow adds to the total return on the investment made.

Here is how the four drivers of real estate wealth work together to produce high returns. Appreciation gradually increases the value. Leverage steepens the return as a percentage of what you invested. Amortization lowers the amount percentage you own simultaneously, and positive cash flow is like a dividend on the top. The longer this process is allowed to continue, the greater the wealth that is built.

Cash flow is a simple calculation and one that is very important for any investor to understand. It is, however, not necessary to find a positive cash flow property in order to make outstanding returns. Properties can be bought that are negative cash flow, and be turned into positive cash flow using strategies discussed later. First, let's learn how to crunch numbers.

10 | Do the Math

With the software and tools available at Own America.com, you can calculate the profitability of an investment property pretty easily, but that is like skipping math classes as a kid and just getting a calculator. It's important to understand the numbers first, and then you can feel free to let the computer do the work for you.

The first calculation you need to internalize is how to determine if a property will lose money (negative cash flow), break even, or make money (positive cash flow) on an annual basis. When you acquire a unit of investment real estate, you are buying an asset that someone will pay you to use. You own it, they live in it. Everybody wins, especially you.

The key numbers are the same as the profit and loss statement of a business, or a household budget:

Gross Income – Expenses = Net Income (Cash Flow)

Annual Gross Income

How much rental revenue is generated, or could be generated by the subject property? If the unit is already occupied by a tenant, this is no more complicated than getting a copy of the lease to see *exactly* how much they pay in rent. If the unit(s) are vacant, then you need to do some homework to determine what the market rent is. This is where a good real estate agent can be enormously helpful. They can tell you the answer in minutes, and they have the incentive to be accurate because they hope you will hire them to find a tenant, and so they need to be right. Once you have established what the Gross Rent will be, you have to account for vacancy. If the unit is currently vacant, you need time to find a tenant, and no rent will be collected while you do that. If the property is occupied, the current tenant may leave at the end of his lease term, at which time the rent stops until you find a replacement. If you don't have a clue what to use as a vacancy rate, start with an assumption of 4.2 percent, which represents one month of vacancy every other year. Subtract that percentage from the total Gross Rent to establish what your Effective Gross Income will be. In other words, how much are you *actually* going to be taking in?

Let's work through these calculations with a simple example of a two-family house.

Purchase Price:	***$750,000***
Effective Gross Income:	
Annual Gross Income	
Unit 1	*$32,000*
Unit 2	*$30,000*
Total Gross Income	*$62,000*
Vacancy 4.2%	*$2,600 (1 month every 2 years)*
Effective Gross Income =	***$59,400***

Operating Expenses

How much does it cost to maintain and operate this property? Included in a properties Operating Expenses are things such as:

- Property taxes.

- Insurance.

- Attorney and accounting fees.

- Property management.

- Repairs and maintenance.

- Snow removal, trash removal, lawn care.

- Rental commissions.

- Utilities.

Operating expenses *do not* include mortgage payments (they fall under Debt Service) because they are not a cost to operate, but a cost to acquire the property. Also not included are capital improvements, such as replacing windows or a new roof. Both of these categories of costs are subtracted *after* you establish what the Net Operating Income will be.

Net Operating Income (NOI)

The clearest way to understand NOI is how much money the property generates before the mortgage is paid. Properties with stable rents and efficient operations are more profitable than properties that are costly to operate and have unreliable or low-rental income. NOI is a way that professional investors can quickly compare and contrast different investment property opportunities.

Effective Gross Income	*$59,400*
— *Operating Expenses*	*$15,400*
NOI	*$44,000*

It boils down to this: If I purchased this asset, how much income will it generate on the basis of rent minus expense? In this example, the answer is $44,000. Now we can establish that as a percentage so we can compare it to other properties that may be larger or smaller, or different types. This is known as the Capitalization Rate.

Capitalization Rate ("Cap Rate")

If I place my capital into service with this investment, what percentage return will I get on a current basis? Cap Rate is calculated by dividing the NOI by the Market Value (or purchase price).

NOI	*$44,000*
Divided by Purchase Price	*$750,000*
= Cap Rate	*5.9%*

This investment will be generating a 5.9 percent annual return on my capital, not including appreciation. Another way to look at it is if I pay $750,000 cash for the property, I would receive a NOI of $44,000, or 5.9 percent. The higher the Cap Rate, the better the return. If I am able to buy this property for less than $750,000, my Cap Rate will go up. I got the same return while paying less for it, which is a better investment.

Appraisers will evaluate similar properties that have recently sold to establish what the Market Cap Rate is for the area at any given time. What are other investors insisting on as a return on their capital? If the market cap rate is 7 percent in the area, the property should sell for a price closer to $630,000. Market Value is calculated by dividing the NOI by the Market Cap Rate.

NOI	*$44,000*
Divided by Market Cap Rate	*7%*
= Market Value	*$630,000*

If the financial details are not available for comparable properties, such as accurate information on the rental income and operating expenses, the Market Cap Rate is subjective and should not be relied upon exclusively. You own personal objectives and desired return is the most important determining factor as to whether a property is the right investment for you.

Debt Service

Of all residential properties bought as investments today, 52 percent are purchased with a mortgage. The principal and interest payments are called Debt Service and are incorporated at this stage to calculate an investor's actual cash income and Return On Investment (ROI). There are several methods for calculating ROI.

Cash-on-Cash Return

After the NOI is established and Debt Service is subtracted from it, what remains is Cash Flow.

NOI	*$44,000*
Minus Debt Service	*$34,000*
= Cash Flow	*$10,000*

In this example, the $750,000 property is acquired with a down payment of $225,000 (30 percent) and a mortgage of $525,000. The mortgage payments equal $34,000/year and leave $10,000 in positive Cash Flow. Cash-on-Cash Return is calculated by dividing the Cash Flow by the investor's down payment.

Cash Flow	$10,000
Divided by Down Pymt	$225,000
= Cash-on-Cash Return	4.44%

In other words, I used $225,000 of my money to buy this asset, and after I rent it out, pay the operating expenses, and pay the mortgage, I have $10,000 in bottom-line profit. That represents a 4.44 percent annual return on my $225,000, not including appreciation.

All of the calculations we have done until now have been static, meaning they are accurate this year and may be accurate next year, but rents and expenses will change. Next we have to add the dimension of time to our analysis.

Internal Rate of Return (IRR)

This is where the rubber meets the road. What is the aggregated return of all cash flows, appreciation, and equity built through paying down principal? The IRR calculation incorporates all of these factors into an annual percentage return on the investment. The IRR can be compared to other forms of investment, such as a mutual fund or savings account, to compare the results using a single percentage rate. Typically, more risky investments will potentially produce a higher rate of return, and more secure investments produce a lower rate of return. This is precisely why real estate investing is so lucrative. Real estate is a stable and reliable asset if purchased and managed right. It is secure, and yet it produces relatively high rates of return.

Before we can dig into calculating future value and appreciation, we need to dig into strategy. The smartest and most successful real estate moguls I've worked with are never satisfied to simply ride the cycle. They insist on an extra boost of value, and there are many ways they accomplish this. This is where you will unleash your creativity, and start looking for that golden opportunity sitting there in plain sight.

11 | The Ugliest Ducklings Become the Loveliest Swans

Real estate is like a snowstorm. No two snowflakes are exactly alike. Every piece of real estate is different than every other, and they are all progressing at their own pace through the Renewable Property Lifecycle. We discussed previously that there is a market cycle churning constantly, moving with the ebbs and flows of supply and demand, presenting opportunities to investors who understand it. The Renewable Property Lifecycle is also churning along, and it is unique to each piece of real estate.

Consider two-single family homes that sit side-by-side on Maple Street, USA. They were built by the same builder at the same time with the same design and finishes. They may have even painted them the same color. With the exception of the precise location, they are exactly the same, until someone moves in. Then each begins its cycle of deterioration/ restoration/deterioration that can span a century or more. The original kitchens, baths, appliances, carpets, and wall coverings are worn out on a different schedule, and repaired or replaced with different materials at different levels of quality by different contractors at different times. Even with two houses that start out identical, after day one, nothing is ever the same. Investors who understand that they can apply their creativity to envisioning changes to a property can materialize value in the same ways professional do.

Change in Condition

Depending on where you are in the market cycle, a property in need of renovation could be valued at significantly less than a comparable property in move-in condition. For example, in the hot market of 2002–2006, buyers were most interested in finding a property with "good bones" in the right location. It did not concern them that they would have to invest further in the property to renovate it because they perceived that the value would continue to increase (forever) and they would make their money back. As human nature often illustrates, people perceive that things will continue as they are forever.

The same is true today in a down market, but from the opposite perspective. People believe real estate values may never go back up again. Most are unwilling to buy real estate that needs improvement because they see it as flushing money down the toilet. In a down market, everyone wants "turn key," so a property in need of repair will likely sit on the market and languish. A languishing property can become stigmatized, as in "something must be wrong with it if it's been on the market for so long," All of this contributes to it becoming devalued, or available to buy for a price that is less than the cost of a comparable house in good condition, minus the cost to renovate. Translation: you can get it cheaper than it's worth.

Change in Tenancy

In the case of rental property, it gets even more appealing. Apartments in excellent condition command higher rents than similar ones in poor condition. This is understood intuitively. A couple looking for a one-bedroom in an area will see two of the same size and description, and be willing to pay more for the one in better shape. Higher rents mean better cash flow, which, in turn, increases value.

An investor in today's market who finds a property in need of upgrading that is occupied by tenants at rental rates consummate with the poor condition of the apartments can increase the value twice by making the repairs and raising the rental income.

There are many cases where landlords have been renting their apartments and have not increased the rents in many years. Sometimes this is due to a relationship with a long-term tenant, and other times it is due to simply being out of touch with the market. Buying a property that is underperforming in terms of the rental income and remedying that is one way the pros create value.

Adaptive Re-use

Professional real estate investors are like magicians, not just in the way they manifest wealth out of thin air, but in the way they don't share their secrets. In the show business of magic, it is referred to as the Magicians' Code, and 99.99 percent of them adhere to it, but once in a while, you will find one who wants everyone to know how magic really works and he lets the cat out of the bag.

I am that guy in real estate investing. It isn't a code with real estate moguls as much as a desire to protect trade secrets. *How* and *where* real estate moguls finds their gems is the lifeblood of their mogul-ness. One thing they will all admit to is that these diamonds in the rough are hiding in plain sight. They are right there, in your town and on your way to work—non-descript opportunities that are just waiting to be uncovered.

If properties were people, they would be crying out to these creative geniuses to save them, to envision them with a higher purpose, nurture their potential, and to make it happen. In fact, one very common trait among real estate moguls is their attribution of human traits to their favorite properties. Invariably, their favorites are the ones they saved.

Real estate moguls ask, "What could this building be?" Or more likely, "What does it want to be?" The application of this strategy is known as Adaptive Re-use: to change a property for the better and use it differently. Here are some examples, large to small:

Case Study: Hudson River Stage

The property at One Point Street in Yonkers, New York was a turn-of-the-19th-century factory that was built on the bank of the Hudson River in the late 1800s when the greatest population center in our nation, the Northeast, was just developing. The waterfronts of America's urban rivers were utilized for the easy access they offered to shipping, as railroads were still young at the time. What was manufactured at this particular factory changed many times during the decades, until eventually it was taken out of service in the 1990s after a 50-year stint as a manufacturing plant for electrical cable. Needless to say, there weren't many environmental laws on the books in the late 1800s, so for a very long time, the plant simply dumped or buried byproducts of their manufacturing activities. The site was a terribly polluted industrial site that was sitting on 23 acres of prime waterfront real estate 20 minutes from Manhattan.

The owner, a multinational industrial giant, contacted my dear friend and mentor, Paul Adler, to handle the case of selling the property. Paul, being a top-tier expert in development and Adaptive Re-use, was the man for the job, and he began by asking the big question: What could it be?

The obvious answer was waterfront condominiums, with awesome views of the Palisades across the Hudson, and the Manhattan skyline to the south. Paul used to say that the Palisades views had not changed one bit since Henry Hudson sailed up the river for the first time. There is also a train station with a 20-minute direct train to Grand Central Station. It could not be a better fit, except for the pollution. A property that was polluted for 100 years needs to be cleaned up before it can be sold and repurposed for residential use. Technically, the property had a negative value in the $100 million range, due to the projected cost of litigation and cleanup.

The negotiations for a cleanup of this magnitude are enormous and usually hostile. State and federal environmental regulators, environmental non-profit watchdog groups, local government, and the chain of corporate owners of the property all lock horns when deciding how much this is going to cost, to whose standards it will be cleaned, and who is going to pay. It looked like a 10-year process at minimum (other environmentally compromised sites have languished for much longer as the parties fight it out in court) so Paul began thinking about ways to generate rental income while the process drudged along and started asking a new question: What could it be while the environmental issues were being worked out?

Let me now describe the site so you get a feel for the task. It is a 23-acre parcel of land with 17 buildings ranging in age from 150 to 40 years old. The most recent use was electrical cable manufacturing, and on the site is a special-purpose building designed for testing newly made cable. This is no chicken-wire fencing. We are talking about high-tension cable designed to carry huge electrical loads across long distances. The testing facility, known as the Blue Box, had the footprint of half a football field, was 11 stories tall, with no interior walls or posts, had 5-foot-thick concrete walls, and all the electrical power needed to test the cable. We used to joke that you could launch a space shuttle with all that juice, or just park it inside. It was that big and wide open.

A few weeks later, it was all over the news that Mayor Rudy Giuliani had a spat with some major motion picture players about building a film studio in the old Brooklyn Navy Yard, and that was the spark that gave Paul the idea that launched the Hudson River Stage. Paul made contact with the Hollywood people and they leapt at the opportunity. Paul secured special permits to use the Blue Box as a film production studio, and during a five-year period while the environmental negotiations took place, the building was leased out to production studios to produce everything from music videos, to commercials, to major feature films.

The best part of this story is that, in addition to collecting high rents for years from a happy film industry, the presence of Hollywood added a sex appeal that made the environmental negotiations go more smoothly. Not that everyone was star struck, but the creative ingenuity of Paul's solution made everyone want to be part of it. The environmental cleanup negotiations went exceedingly well, and the cleanup itself was completed ahead of schedule.

The conversion of a factory to a film studio is an extreme example of Adaptive Re-use as applied on a large scale by a true real estate mogul, but it illustrates the potential creativity that can be applied to solve impossible problems and create value. How can this concept be applied a little closer to home?

Case Study: 54 North Broadway

It's true that my personal experience revolves around a few specific regions of the country; specifically the New York area and the Southeast United States. I want to provide concrete examples of these strategies so you can adapt the example to a marketplace near you. In the next case study, we found a completely different situation that had the potential for another kind of adaptive re-use strategy. The property at 54 North Broadway is a Victorian mansion in Tarrytown, New York in a great location. It was purchased and renovated by the previous owner who planned to sell it at top dollar when he completed his work. The building is three stories tall and has residential apartments on the second and third floors, and an office on the first. The previous owner lived on the second floor and used the first for his business. The location was conducive to office use, being on the main commercial street in town, so we wondered if the office component of the building could be expanded.

A review of the zoning at Town Hall gave us the answer we were hoping for. Each local municipality has control over its own zoning code, and uses the code to define what types of real estate can be built where, and what it can be used for. Certain areas or streets are reserved for residential use, and others for retail stores, office buildings, or industrial complexes. Often, a center of a small town will have zoning that allows for mixed use, typically residential and retail or office. You've seen these buildings—a store or office downstairs and apartments upstairs.

In the case of 54 North Broadway, the building was originally a home, and the zoning was changed many years ago to allow for mixed use. The second floor is where the gold was. The building had an allowable use of office on the first floor, office *or* residential on the second, and residential on the third. In other words, it was allowable to switch the second floor to office space. Because that space would rent for about $2,000/month as an apartment, but the office would rent for $3,000/month, the rent would increase by $12,000/year. This translates into a significantly better cash flow and return on investment, which in turn translates into a higher value.

This building was modified by filing a few forms, attending a few meetings, and securing a renewed permit in the village to use the second floor as office. Before a coat of paint was put on the walls, the building was worth more.

The Simplest Application of Adaptive Re-use

Do a little research in a neighborhood near you. Search for sale prices of three- and four-bedroom homes. You will often find a disparity of value between the two of roughly 20 percent, meaning a three-bedroom house would be worth $400,000 and a four-bedroom on the same block would be worth $500,000. Then search for three-bedroom houses with a den and you should see the price is close to the standard three-bedroom price.

The difference between a den and a bedroom is basically the presence of a closet. I bought a three-bedroom house with an office and converted the office to a fourth bedroom. The value increased 20 percent for having done nothing but *remove* built-in counters. There was a closet, so I had an instant bedroom.

Adaptive Re-use: Imagination + Execution = Increased value

12 | MARKET INTELLIGENCE: FIND A RISING TIDE

A re you a real estate enthusiast? Do you:

- read the news stories about the housing market first?

- hear a conversation at a party about real estate and mosey over to get in on it?

- feel a deep pride of ownership (if you own your home) and think of your home as a member of your family?

- go on vacation and pick up real estate magazines for day-dreaming inspiration?

If you are a real estate enthusiast, you don't need my silly test to prove it. You already know it, and therefore you will love doing the research for real estate investments. Searching for a diamond in the rough that is right under everyone's nose is very exciting. In fact, every successful real estate mogul I've met started as an enthusiast, and the market research is the part many love the most.

The correct approach to picking a winning real estate investment is top-down. First you find a market where the tide is rising, and then you find a property that fits your situation. So strap on your seat belt and let's take a look at the big picture to see where the winners are.

Sometimes the driver of change in the Renewable Property Lifecycle has nothing to do with the property at all, but where it's located. This can take the form of an uplifting momentum of a place going through a turnaround, where all boats rise with the tide, or it can be the opposite— a place that you need to avoid.

When we hear of governments that are anti-business, it's usually at the state level. States compete for corporations. The most competitive states provide tax incentives and streamlined regulations in order to bring jobs, taxes, and prestige to their state. The least competitive states create obstacles, such as onerous regulations, endless bureaucracy, and high taxes. On the local level, however, it's all about awnings and nature paths.

A few towns away from 54 North Broadway is another village with a very similar appeal: suburban communities with charming downtowns, a sense of identity, and train stations that bring people to the city. But this other town has a chip on its shoulder.

This small village has made life more difficult on its businesses through a series of decisions that has kept the village from improving. The place where this happens in a town is sometimes called the planning board.

My first experience with this planning board was nine years ago when our company expanded to a new region, and we began opening real estate branch offices.

I found a great location in the "gateway" to the town. This is the entrance to the town where Broadway and two other main streets converge. In the center of town, there were positive changes happening. A car dealership and a gas station relocated, and the land was cleared for redevelopment. It was good news because they took up a lot of space, and both would do better located in a busy commercial district rather than a small, quaint village. Plus, land purposed for automotive use is usually dirty and diminishes the quaintness of a downtown village.

One investor bought the gas station land and drew up plans for a small bank-like office building. He wanted to build it for a buyer and sell it to them. *It was perfect for us!* But it got rejected. The board determined that it was part of the "gateway" to town and, therefore, needed to be included in the master plan, which called for a small inn with a quaint bed and breakfast vibe. The owner could not make that work. There was no real demand for an inn, and so it sits as a vacant lot to this day, with the owner paying the taxes and not collecting income.

I moved on and found another perfect opportunity with a building at the center of town. The old library was for sale, which was owned by the village. Our real estate offices are nice and compliment the architecture of the town, but they are not as cool as an ice cream shop, book store, or cafe. We understand, but it's a free country, right?

Sort of. Our bid was rejected because the board thought an art gallery would be better for the common good. That building remains vacant and boarded up at the time of this writing, eight years after we were rejected! The art gallery was apparently not a viable business after all.

We wound up striking out on buildings for sale, but we found a great store to rent, which goes against my personal philosophy to own rather than rent, but my last interaction with the village board was just an application for a new awning over the front windows. It was rejected on the grounds that it was not "village-y" enough. So I added stripes, and now the real estate office looks like an ice cream shop.

I know this sounds like we were blacklisted and they were trying to keep us out, but they weren't. They did this to everyone in town. I'm not going to tell you the name of this little piece of heaven, but there might be one lurking near you.

You need to know which towns are going to hurt you and which are going to help you. The best way to find out is to attend the planning board meetings in a town you are considering investing in. They are published on the town's Website and open to the public. You don't need to say a word to anyone. Just listen. You will be able to gauge if they are positive, neutral, or negative. Anything but negative is workable.

A final note: remember the car dealer that relocated and was the cornerstone of the "gateway" to town? The owner wanted to build a parking lot for the town, which would have generated parking revenues and helped all the stores and citizens in town. The board wanted a nature trail. It remains a vacant lot 10 years later. Everyone loses.

Find Your Florida

I use Florida as a metaphor for a perfect real estate-buying opportunity. The market there is taking a beating during the recession. So many people lost their shirts in Florida real estate during the past several years that you'd think I was losing my mind, but let's do the analysis.

What are the reasons that Florida is in such a bad situation? Bad behavior, on several fronts. Developers, speculators, lenders, and consumers came together to create a poop-storm of bad decisions.

Developers built like mad. At one point during the boom, I was visiting my brother Dan at the University of Miami and looked out my hotel window to see a skyline bristling with cranes. I counted them and there were 23 cranes in all. It was quite a sight, and a testament to how much money was being poured into that city. Then I counted the tall buildings (the ones that were already built), and found 15. This city was growing from a skyline of 15 high-rises to a skyline of 38, and they were mostly luxury condo towers. By 2005, 69,000 new condo units were either under construction or planned in Miami.

Each one of those developers represented a risk-taker who was betting on demand for Miami real estate to skyrocket in order to support so many new housing units. The very first few buildings that went on sale sold out so quickly that it attracted the rest of the pack, backed by hedge funds, lenders, and other sources of capital. There was a problem, though. Half of the buyers of those condos were not owner/occupants, but speculators.

Speculators are investors who do not intend to add any value to an asset they acquire. They simply hope to profit from timing market fluctuations. They thrive on volatility, and when they are amateurs, they can cause havoc. The rapid appreciation of Florida real estate was a bright light that attracted speculators at all experience levels who shared a common "business plan." If this plan was even written down it was probably on the back of a cocktail napkin; buy and flip a new luxury condo the moment the construction was completed. After all, there would always be a hoard of buyers who would be willing to pay $600,000 for a condo they know was purchased for $475,000 eight months earlier!

In real estate, the term absorption refers to how the market will soak up new supply. In other words, the 69,000 newly built condos would need to be absorbed by the market. Speculators do not absorb units, they pass them along. Someone has to move in for a unit to be truly absorbed. It has been reported that more than half of these condos in Miami were sold to speculators who put them right back on the market, which means the market needed to absorb an additional 34,500 condos. That's more than 100,000 units hitting the market in the same cycle. All of those units needed to sell and resell for prices to remain stable, but the boom ran out of steam. Thousands of speculators found themselves with big mortgage payments and no one to rent their condos.

The lenders who made those mortgages simply lost their minds. It has been a known fact in the lending industry forever that owner/occupants are more reliable risks than investors, because if someone can only make one payment this month, they are making it on their home. Therefore, investor mortgages were harder to get. Investment borrowers were always required to put at least 25 percent down and prove every penny of their income and assets to get a loan. But Wall Street pushed, borrowers pulled, and government relaxed lending policies to the point where investors could get a no-money-down investment mortgage without showing the bank a pay stub to prove their income.

The result is massive amount of foreclosures, half-built high rises, and property values in rapid decline. It would be a reasonable conclusion that Florida is a horrible place in which to invest—but it would be the wrong conclusion.

Ask yourself this: why has Florida's economy been growing for the past 40 years? The answer is simple: climate and demographics. People from the population centers in the Northeast retire and move south, and the places where they tend to go are down the eastern seaboard. This migration trend is the reason Florida's population has been skyrocketing for decades. There is nothing to indicate that it is slowing down. On the contrary, 72 million Baby Boomers are entering their retirement ages, and the highest percentage of them live in the Northeast.

Think of the market conditions in Florida as a forest fire: terrifying, deadly, the most destructive force on earth. Now picture a glacier creeping toward it. As violent and furious as the forest fire is, what will happen when the glacier gets there? The glacier wins every time.

The migration of Baby Boomers is the glacier, and there is no question that it will put out that forest fire. It won't happen tomorrow, but it will happen.

Florida has a short-term problem, but a fantastic future. Situations like this exist all over the country. Sometimes they are high-profile like this, but usually they are obscure. Find *your* Florida.

Find Your Seabrook Island

Let's take a deeper dive into this same migration pattern to see another opportunity hiding in plain sight. On the front end of the Florida migration decades ago were the early adopters who are no longer Yankees, but full fledged Floridians by now. And guess who they think are ruining Florida? The Yankees (not the baseball team). It's getting too crowded, too overdeveloped. They need to find a new place, so they are coming halfway back.

They are affectionately known as half-backs. People are fleeing Florida to get away from New Yorkers and to find a quieter existence, and they are finding it in the Carolinas. The Carolinas are not experiencing the same pain as Florida, but then, they didn't experience the meteoric rise in prices, and didn't overdevelop or overspeculate during the boom. The Carolinas are growing steadily for some very good reasons; quality of life, cost of living, scenic beauty, economic development, and Southern hospitality.

Within the larger market of the Carolinas is the City of Charleston, a port city that was a central economic driver of our nation for the first century of our existence. Since then, it has become a quaint, vibrant, historic city that attracts tourist, half-backs, and companies who want to relocate to a new and better place.

A few years ago, I was researching the Carolinas and found Charleston, and within the Charleston area I found a little ugly duckling called Seabrook Island. A barrier island south of the city, Seabrook had seen better days. The island, which is private and gated, had beach club and golf amenities that sorely needed an upgrade. On my first visit there, I sat by the pool getting bit by flies. I loved it. Did you ever think that flies could suppress property values? They do when they are part of a maintenance problem that spoils the experience. The flies were the first clue that something very fixable was wrong.

Seabrook's neighbor to the north, Kiawah Island, is the lovely swan that sits less than a mile away from where I was being attacked by filthy bugs. Things were very different on Kiawah. The island had just finished construction of the five-star Sanctuary Hotel and Golf Resort, which hosted presidents, kings, and PGA golf events. Kiawah's brand was on the rise, and real estate values were climbing as more and more of the rich and famous discovered the charms of the Charleston coast. Real estate values on Kiawah were double what they were on Seabrook, despite the fact that they shared the same ocean, beaches, location, and southern vibe. All the important things were the same.

Up the road, where the entrance gates of the two islands split off at the fork, a ground breaking was taking place. A new shopping area was being built, and this was no strip mall. It was to be called Freshfields Village, and it would have a market, restaurants, high-end stores, and a village atmosphere. The developers did something ingenious. They hired five architectural firms to design the concept, and split the 50 lots up among them, but mixed them all up. No architect had any adjacent lots, and they were not allowed to talk to each other or coordinate their designs. The idea was to build a town that looked like it had been developed over a century, as opposed to being master-planned. Nothing matched, and it turned out awesome!

As an investor, this means a lot to me. Someone believed that Kiawah was on the rise and build a five-star resort. Someone else thought that a quaint shopping district could be supported by these islands, built 50 stores, and went to great expense to make it special. Sometimes you just need to follow the money. Kiawah was a safe bet, but I had my eye on the ugly stepsister.

A closer look next door at Seabrook Island revealed that the maintenance issues were a result of the Seabrook Island Club's financial problems. Their business model was failing. They had previously been generating revenue from rental commissions and property management fees for the vacation villas on the island, but closed that business for lack of profitability. The Island needed a new business model. Then the Board of Directors proposed a new rule. If you buy real estate on the island, you *must* join the club. They called it Island One and they projected that the revenue generated would solve their problems. The residents enthusiastically voted for and passed the initiative.

With a steady flow of new members, revenues jumped immediately. Then the club made another fateful decision to reenter the real estate business, but instead of doing vacation rentals and property management, they would focus on real estate sales. They started Seabrook Island Real Estate and became the dominant real estate broker on the Island with 80 percent market share. Of course, the residents used the real estate company owned by their club. None of them liked being bitten by flies, so they had a vested interest in making the club, and all its derivative businesses, a success.

Five years later, the Seabrook Island Club tore down the beach and golf club buildings and built stunning new facilities. The investment I made in Seabrook Island in 2005 is up 45 percent despite the real estate crisis because it was an undervalued asset. Today, Seabrook real estate continues to close the gap with Kiawah. Until the two islands are valued the same, Seabrook has unrealized upside.

In the end, the problems on Seabrook were obvious and solvable, and the trends were very encouraging. In the Carolinas, in Charleston, and right next door on Kiawah, the economic tides were rising. Seabrook solved its problems and is rising even faster to catch up. The ugly ducking emerged a lovely swan.

One more thing. This was the property that was a three-bedroom with an office when I bought it. I converted it to a four-bedroom, and it is one of only three that are available for rent on the island. Not only did the value jump, but the rent has gone up every year since I bought it. Value is all around you, if you know how to find it.

Find Your Newburgh

In Chapter 14, I share the strategy I call "have a kid, buy a condo," which is an example of a long-term investment strategy. I purchased a condo as an investment for my daughter's college fund. I chose that particular condo because the price point was where I wanted it, starting at about $200,000 and ending up at about $400,000 by the time it's time to send my daughter to college. It was the ideal choice because of where this condo is located. It's an hour from my house, which is reachable when needed, but far enough away for me to want it to be as turn key as possible. A brand new condo hit the mark on both counts. Condos are typically priced at the entry level of a market for first-time homebuyers and empty nesters. There are exceptions obviously, such as luxury waterfront or downtown high-rises, but in the case of Newburgh, New York, condos were priced lower than houses.

Condos are also lower maintenance than houses because you technically own from the walls in. The roof, driveway, backyard (such as it is), storm drains, walkways, and so on are not typically your responsibility to maintain. You pay for the maintenance of the exterior in one simple payment that you consider part of your monthly payment to own. A brand new condo is even more turn-key because everything is new. If the washer and dryer are supposed to last five years, you have that long before you have to take the phone call that "the dryer broke and I need to do laundry!" The same goes for the fridge, electrical work, plumbing, and so on.

The market for condos as rentals is also pretty easy to research. Are there a lot of apartment complexes in the area that compete with it? Are there a lot of condos for rent in this complex that compete with it? What are they all charging in rent? These are all simple questions that a local real estate agent can answer accurately and easily.

In the case of Newburgh, there are not very many apartment complexes, and the ones that do exist are not huge. Also, the employment base is pretty stable in the area. Everything is looking good, and this combination of attributes is not uncommon. There are some towns in every area that lend themselves well to rentals. But Newburgh has something else going for it; something extra that made it worthwhile for me to go outside the 10-mile radius of home and venture an hour away.

Just a few miles away is Stewart Airport. Stewart Airport was a small air strip at the turn of the last century. Subsequently it was donated in 1930 to the Town of Newburgh to become a municipal airport, but in 1941, when the war effort needed it, it was sold to the government to become part of West Point Military Academy (a few miles away) for the price of $1.

In 1994, Stewart Air Force Base was privatized and became Stewart International Airport, the fourth international airport in the metro New York area. Under private ownership, Stewart had many starts and stops as its various owners and local government bodies struggled to find the right purpose, mission, and business model to make it a commercial success and attract the passenger and freight traffic necessary to support a viable airport. The airport was never a commercial success, to the disappointment of the local community.

In 2007, the fate of Stewart was sealed when the Port Authority of New York and New Jersey took the property over. The Port Authority owns the other big three: JFK, LaGuardia and Newark Airports, and the demand for passenger flights was so high that the system was overloaded and could not keep up with it. The Port Authority's plan is to gradually move freight traffic away from the Big Three to Stewart, freeing up air space for more passenger traffic, and directly addressing the problem with a solution that would work.

In other words, Stewart is poised to become a major freight airport, which means a rising economic tide for everyone in the region. Jobs will be created, which means tenants will be created.

How do you pick a winning market? Start with the big-picture approach. Find out what the big players are doing. Find out who else has committed their money and is betting on population growth in the area. Home Depot and Lowes don't open stores on a whim. They do enormous research on population trends, demographics, and traffic patterns. They are important to watch in particular because they are in the home improvement business, which means they are targeting areas where people will be putting money into upgrading and enhancing real estate. You don't need a huge team of highly skilled market researchers. You can use theirs.

13 | SET THE TABLE

Buying one piece of investment real estate can be a life-changing decision. Because of the dynamics of how equity is built, the power of this asset class is unrivaled. If this book accomplishes anything, I hope that it will be to eliminate the barriers that keep millions of people from using real estate as a wealth-building vehicle. This chapter is about identifying those barriers and obliterating them. By this point, you should want real estate in your portfolio pretty badly. What might be holding you back?

Research overwhelmingly shows that most Americans understand intuitively that real estate is the best long-term investment. A recent study by Gallup illustrated the phenomenon.

Which of the following do you think is the best long-term investment?

Gallup Poll, April 6-9, 2009

The researchers concluded:

There has been some recovery in perceptions of real estate as the best long-term investment—it dipped to a low of 26 [percent] last September but now is at 33 [percent]. Americans may believe that the housing market is beginning to pick back up. A separate question in the poll found 71 [percent] saying now is a good time to buy a house, up 18 points from a year ago and the highest since 2005.

But even with the improvement this year, housing still ranks well below where it did during the real estate boom years—in 2002, 50 percent of Americans said housing was the best long-term investment.

Subgroup Differences

Americans' perceptions of the best long-term investment vary to some degree, depending on their demographic characteristics. For example, upper-income respondents are most likely to view real estate as the best investment, while lower-income respondents choose savings accounts. Middle-income Americans are equally divided between savings accounts and real estate.

**Views of the best long-term investment
by annual household income**

Gallup Poll

Men and women also differ as to which of the four is the best investment in the long run, with men most likely to say real estate and women savings accounts.

Views of the best long-term investment by gender

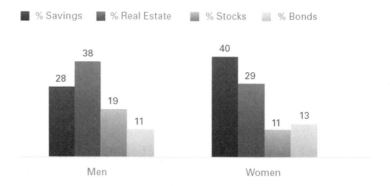

■ % Savings ■ % Real Estate ■ % Stocks ■ % Bonds

Gallup Poll

This poll reflects something we all sense. So what percentage of the people who believe real estate is the best long-term investment are taking action on that belief?

Another poll released by Gallup measures the sources of income people are depending on to secure their retirement.

When you retire, how much do you expect to rely on each of the following sources of money? Will it be a major source of income, a minor source of income, or not a source at all?

	2007	2010	Change (pct. pts.)
Social Security	27	34	7
Money from an inheritance	8	9	1
Other savings, such as a regular savings account or CDS	23	22	-1
Annuities or other insurance plans	9	8	-1
Rent and royalties	7	6	-1
Part-time work	21	18	-3
Individual stock or stock mutual fund investments	24	20	-4
A 401(k), IRA, Keogh or other retirement savings account	52	45	-7
A work-sponsored pension plan	31	23	-8
The equity you have built up in your home	30	20	-10

There are so many things I find interesting in this study.

First, the real estate is represented twice in the list of choices, under "Rent and royalties" and "The equity you have built up in your home." During the boom year of 2007, 30 percent of the respondents were relying on home equity, which dropped dramatically by 2010. People's faith in a long-term investment was shaken by a short-term drop in value. Second, the question is about retirement *income*, and yet, rents received the lowest rating.

Third, the study has a blind spot. The question does not give the option of "the equity I have built up in my investment properties."

Fourth, "social security" and "money from an inheritance" are the only two categories that grew during the recession. How scary is it that so many people are depending on the government or their parents to take care of them when they retire?

This research is consistent with what I have experienced as a guy who has spent his life in all aspects of the real estate business. Most people know that the best way to get wealthy is in real estate, and too few ever do anything about it.

You Believe in Real Estate Investing, So What's Holding You Back?

When consumers were asked this question in a recent survey by OwnAmerica.com, the responses were as follows:

1. "I don't know how."

2. "I don't have the money."

3. "I don't want to be a landlord."

Let's examine each of these responses and the adjoining obstacle they represent.

"I don't know how."

I get this a lot. It's the reason I wrote this book and started a national advisory firm. People want to learn the real estate investing game, but where do they turn to learn it?

The residential real estate industry is all about homeownership, which makes sense because 80 percent of the residential properties that are bought each year will be occupied by the new owner. Twenty percent of all residential sales are to investors, and there isn't really an organized national industry of professionals to represent it. There are 1 million real estate agents in this country, and 99 percent of them focus on selling homes, not investments.

The multiple listing service, that real estate database that virtually all local real estate agents share, does not have any space for rental income, operating expenses, lease terms, and so on. The database architecture is simply not built for investment properties.

There are several national real estate Websites, such as Realtor.com, with millions of properties on the market for sale, but they are focused on homeownership as well. Until just recently, the online tools for researching markets and properties did not exist. This is why we launched OwnAmerica.com. Check it out.

Then there is the commercial real estate industry. These are the guys and gals that sell office buildings, shopping centers, and gigantic apartment buildings. Surely they could represent residential property as an investment. But they don't.

The asset class of small residential investment property is neither fish nor foul. Do a Google search, and you will see that there is a blind spot.

What about the people who advise their clients on financial planning and investing? They are financial advisors who typically fall into one of the following categories:

1. Accountant/tax advisor.

2. Financial planner: stocks, mutual funds, bonds.

3. Financial planner: life insurance, disability insurance, annuities.

4. Attorney: wills, trusts, estate planning.

There is crossover among this team of professionals, and they tend to agree on some basic pieces of advice: plan for the future, create growth through mostly stable long-term investments, and save on taxes. The products these advisors use are typically passive investments and real estate is not one of them, despite the fact that it is proven to be the most reliable way to achieve the stated goals.

Financial advisors will privately acknowledge real estate as a high-quality asset class, but because it is not their field, the advice ends there. Some financial planners will recommend Real Estate Investment Trusts or REITS (publicly traded commercial real estate ownership), but not individual property ownership.

Most often, financial planners seek to advise their clients on the full spectrum of their financial future, but direct them to products they specialize in and are compensated for. This is not a critical statement. Those planners are experts in their field. They do not know real estate investing, so they stick to their knitting, just as I should never give a stock pick or recommend an insurance policy.

To sum it up, residential real estate sells homes, commercial real estate represents corporations, real estate Websites show pretty pictures, and financial advisors sell paper investments.

Prospective investors have nowhere to turn, and too often, they turn to the "get rich quick" gurus who write books, record audio programs, and sell them on late night television and the Internet. These gurus are not in the real estate investment business. They are in the "direct response marketing" business. Their business model is closer to companies that sell exercise equipment and skin care through direct response marketing than to an investment advisory profession.

The direct response marketing business requires a hook: "lose weight fast," "take wrinkles away like magic," "get rich quick with no money down." The hook makes the phone ring and their telemarketing rep closes the sale. Successful use of the product is not necessary for short-term success. This explains why so many marketeers in these categories disappear after a short while, and why they are soon replaced by a new marketeer with the same hook. Hooks work to make the call center's phones ring, but you can't lose weight fast without hard work and discipline, you won't make wrinkles disappear with cream, and you absolutely will not get rich quick in real estate.

All you have to do is look at the nature of the real estate crash of the late 2000's to see how dangerous the appeal of "get rich quick" can be.

"I don't have the money."

Admittedly, this is a major obstacle. Low down payment mortgages are not available for investment real estate. Lenders are well aware that the credit risk of an investor is much greater than that of an owner/occupant. Borrowers are more likely to pay the mortgage on their home than their investment if they are forced to make a choice. Decades of loan performance analysis proves this, which makes you wonder why lenders ignored this and gave so many low down payment loans to investors during the Roaring 2000s.

Positive cash flow is a very important element in the power of real estate to create wealth. Putting down a large down payment is one of the reasons a property will produce positive cash flow. If you put 10 or 20 percent down, your mortgage is significantly larger than if you put 30 percent down. Bigger mortgage means higher payments, which means rental income is less likely to cover the expense to own.

This is one of those situations where it takes money to make money. However, the day an investor begins saving money for a down payment is the day his investment plan begins. For many, the plan does not begin on the day they purchase their first property, but the day they begin to save for it.

There are sources of funds that an investor may not be aware of that can be used for real estate investing. For example, you can buy real estate in your IRA. This is one of the best kept secrets in financial planning for a very simple reason. The industry that manages IRA assets does not sell real estate, so most investors are never given that option by their advisors.

More than 10 trillion dollars are currently held in IRAs. This is a major source of funds for investors that can be tapped. Furthermore, IRA accounts are long-term in nature, which makes them ideal for real estate investing. Most IRA investors understand that they will not touch their IRA until they are 59 1/2 years old. This is the type of long-term perspective that leads to success in real estate investing. There are very specific requirements, however, and you should speak to a Self Directed IRA Custodian to find out more.

"I don't want to be a landlord": Tenants, toilets, and taxes

Imagine a new restaurant opened in your town and in a conversation with the restaurateur, he says, "I can't stand people who are hungry and won't cook for themselves!" Have you ever called tech support and got a technician that seems to resent you for not being able to fix your own computer? What about the telephone operator who gets annoyed because you asked for two numbers, as if to say, "how lazy are you?"

What makes all these examples so frustrating and ridiculous when we encounter them is that we know that these people would not have a job if it weren't for non-cooking, computer-phobic, lazy people who would rather pay $1.50 than open the yellow pages.

We've all seen it at some point or another: A business that hates its customers.

Now, what would you say about a small business owner who had one or two customers that paid hundreds or thousands of dollars each month to the business? You say those customers are always right, and to the business owner, you would say "hug those customers."

Tenants are customers

A landlord is a business owner who purchased an asset that a customer is paying for the use of. The tenant is that customer. The first step to being a great real estate investor is finding love in your heart for your customers.

Granted, managing property and tenant relationships requires time, energy, a file cabinet, writing checks, making deposits, hiring contractors, and taking annoying phone calls at times when the roof springs a leak. Big deal. Show me a small business with this kind of potential that requires no effort.

Once you internalize true appreciation for your tenants, the emphasis must be on finding good ones. This is where a strong real estate agent can be enormously helpful. One of the services he or she will provide is getting authorization from prospective tenants and running credit checks. You don't need to guess whether these folks pay their bills. Bad credit equals a bad tenant. Find another one.

Do a little detective work. Look them up on Google and Facebook. I once found out that a tenant was in a lawsuit with their former landlord. There's a red flag for you. Most of the time, you will confirm the opposite, that they are exactly who they say they are, have real jobs, and are not crazy.

Get a month's rent as a security deposit. If they have a pet, get another half or full month's rent. You will need to do a deep cleaning when Fido moves out.

Be in contact with your tenants. E-mail to thank them for paying the rent on time. When your portfolio gets bigger, this can become a challenge, but it's just like sending birthday cards. It's not required, but it means a lot.

Full occupancy is the objective. Every month without a customer is a bad month. The most important objective is to keep your units occupied. Do that by being market sensitive on rents. Again, a strong real estate agent will earn their keep here. If the market has gotten softer, you will know it by looking at other rentals in your area that are similar to yours. Be realistic about whether yours is better or worse. This is not your home, so there is no reason to take anything personally. Determine how competitive your product is and price it accordingly. Waiting three extra months to get your price is a mistake. For example, a $1,000/month apartment will generate $12,000 a year. If it stays vacant for three months, it generates only $9,000. If the owner lowered the asking rent to $900 and got it rented quickly, the annual rent will be $10,800. That's 20 percent more rent in one year. Better to lower the asking rent, and raise it again when the lease expires, if the market has improved.

A simple tickler file is a must. Your leases should require tenants to give you 60 days' notice if they want to renew. On the 59th day you need to call them to confirm they are leaving, and get on the task of finding a new customer. Do a physical inspection of the place to see whether you need to paint or clean carpets, for example. Line up those services for the week the tenant moves out. Remember, for excessive wear and tear, you have their security deposit.

Hire your real estate agent and get the unit on the market right away for the competitive asking rent.

Toilets

Property maintenance is the second category of "hassle" in running a business that invests in real estate. I am sure restaurateurs complain about having to hire people to wash dishes and sweep floors—or maybe they just understand it as part of the business.

All landlords fall into one of four categories:

1. Do it yourselfers.

2. General contractors.

3. Hands-off.

4. Incompetents.

Do it yourself: If you have this ability, you are better than me, and chances are you are not terribly intimidated by the whole idea of property maintenance. You will see an added benefit in your profitability because you will be trading your time for dollars.

General Contractors: Most successful small investors fall into this category. They have a list of contractors who they trust and have a relationship with. Those contractors value their relationship with the investor because it represents repeat business. Investors who are incompetent can be turned into general contractors fairly easily by building a rolodex of contractors and repairmen. Following is an excerpt from the Investor Profile that can be found at OwnAmerica.com. This part of the profile deals with identifying the weak spots in your property management capabilities.

Landlord Scoring System

On a scale of 1-5 (5 being the highest)

1. Do-it-yourselfer: Are you able to make repairs yourself?

Construction	1	2	3	4	5 (very frequently)
Electrical	1	2	3	4	5
Heating/AC	1	2	3	4	5
Plumbing	1	2	3	4	5
Landscaping	1	2	3	4	5

2. General contractors: Do you have a working relationship with contractors?

Construction contractor	1	2	3	4	5 (very confident)
Electrical contractor	1	2	3	4	5
Heating/AC contractor	1	2	3	4	5

Plumbing

contractor   1   2   3   4   5

Landscaping

contractor   1   2   3   4   5

Everyone who lives indoors has some interaction with repairmen and contractors. Some you like, some you don't, and some categories you have no experience in. After identifying the holes in your roster of contractors, set out to fill them. Ask friends and neighbors for referrals. Make contact with the contractors and take the time to meet them. Inform them of your plans to buy investment properties and ask them if they'd like to be your go-to guys. The worst time to be looking for an electrician is after the lights go out. Set up your team in advance, and you will immediately feel the intimidation factor dissipate.

Hands-off investors need to hire a property manager and pay a fee of 4–5 percent of the annual rental income to the manager. It is possible to make a private arrangement with an individual handyman to deal with basic maintenance issues, and collect the rent as owner. Property managers will do both for their fee. This is a cottage industry made up of small players who operate in each local market across the country. Do the homework, meet the players, check the references, and negotiate a good relationship. By making your investment strategy hands-off, you are giving up some profitability, but it is possible to achieve a clean, turn-key arrangement. Real estate investing is still a business you must be engaged in personally. Property managers will never have the same commitment as the owner.

14 | ENTREPRENEURSHIP REQUIRES VISION: PLAN YOUR STRATEGY

I magine for a moment that you are sitting down with a financial planner to discuss your long-term financial future. Next, imagine that the first thing the financial planner says is, "I like International Semiconductor Inc. It's trading at below-market levels and just released a new product that has been well-received."

Or imagine you are having lunch with an old friend who has recently quit his job to start a business, and he wants to know if you'd be interested in investing in it. You ask for the business plan and he says, "It's going to be awesome. We're going to sell stuff on the Web and make millions."

The equivalent approach to real estate investing would be to wake up one day and decide to invest in real estate, and start looking for properties. Or to hear about a "steal" on a property and decide to become a real estate investor. That's not a strategy, it's a novelty. It would surprise you if you knew how many real estate investors in the last 10 years got the idea to buy a property because they heard their friends talking about it at a party. It would *not* surprise you to learn that these were many of the investors who lost their shirts on short-term flip schemes.

Every business endeavor or long-term financial strategy requires a plan. Real estate investing is no different.

I want to instill in you a deeply rooted commitment to treating real estate as a long-term strategy. You can make money quickly, and I explained how to find undervalued properties and manufacture instant equity, but that does not make you rich. A good buy at the onset of an investment plan does not mean the investment has matured. It simply means you bought well and set yourself up for even greater returns as you ride the cycle forward and mature the investment over time. Said another way, you must buy with the intent to hold. If you decide to flip sooner than planned because the opportunity arises, then do it. Buying to hold insures that you never get caught needing to flip in a market that is not cooperative. Think about all the get-rich-quick artists who bought to flip in the last cycle and could not hold. They were forced to sell at the worst time and took major losses. Follow my advice, and this will not happen to you.

Stephen Covey, author of a book that changed a lot of lives, *The Seven Habits of Highly Effective People*, placed this principal very high on his list, at #2: "Begin with the End in Mind."

"Habit 2 is based on imagination—the ability to envision in your mind what you cannot at present see with your eyes. It is based on the principle that all things are created twice. There is a mental (first) creation, and a physical (second) creation. The physical creation follows the mental, just as a building follows a blueprint. If you don't make a conscious effort to visualize who you are and what you want in life, then you empower other people and circumstances to shape you and your life by default. Begin with the End in Mind means to begin each day, task, or project with a clear vision of your desired direction and destination, and then continue by flexing your proactive muscles to make things happen.

"One of the best ways to incorporate Habit 2 into your life is to develop a Personal Mission Statement. It focuses on what you want to be and do. It is your plan for success. It reaffirms who you are, puts your goals in focus, and moves your ideas into the real world. Your mission statement makes you the leader of your own life. You create your own destiny and secure the future you envision."

Why is this so crucial? Because real estate investing requires patience, attention to details, and a strong stomach when you open the newspaper and see the headline "Housing Meltdown!" When a real estate investment is inextricably linked in your mind to an important life goal, it is much easier to stay the course. When each and every investment you make is assigned to a specific outcome that is important to you, you develop into a great investor. While it is wonderful to buy property that is undervalued and make a score on an investment, it is much more wonderful to do that several times during a lifetime and achieve all your financial dreams as a result. This is not about making a buck, but about amassing a fortune.

Your Real Estate Mission Statement

The first step in developing a clear vision of the financial outcome you want to create with your real estate investment strategy is to answer a few questions about yourself, and begin to set your own expectations.

Start your strategy by dreaming. Dream about your life in 10 or 20 years. How much better do you want it to be than today? What kind of financial success do you want to achieve by then? After all, 10 to 20 years is a long time. You can really make some exciting things take off with a runway that long. If you don't have the money saved yet to make your first investment, or you have debt you must clean up first, that can be the first five years of your plan. *You have time* to build a fortune because you are taking a long view. No one thinks of their future in terms of two to three years, just as no one thinks of a career as a five-year project. A career, a business, and a family are all long-term objectives. You must frame your real estate investment strategy the same way.

You will notice that I talk about retirement throughout this process, which I define as the day you no longer *need* to work. Don't visualize retirement as being put out to pasture on the golf course, unless that is what you love. Think of it as total freedom with your time and energy. No longer required to work for money, you are able to work on what you feel like working on. Do you want to start a foundation when you "retire," continue to grow your company because it's fun, start new businesses, or go fishing/antiquing/traveling and golfing every day?

Retirement equals freedom

- When do you plan on retiring?

- How many years is that from now?

- Do you have kids? What are their names and ages?

- How will you set them up for their future?

- What will it mean for them when you succeed?

- Where do you want to be living when you retire?

- How do you want to be spending your time?

Write your answers to these questions down. When you are finished, close your eyes and picture the future you have described here. Think about how it will make you feel to know you succeeded in making your dream a reality. How will your spouse or significant other look at you? That person loves you for all the right reasons. The fact that you brought home the bacon is just the icing on the cake!

How will the young people in your life look at you, having witnessed your entrepreneurial success firsthand? Remember the impact of Uncle George Parker on Allene Reynolds as a child growing up during the Great Depression. Living in comfort can make for a comfortable life, but living with inspiration creates an inspired life. That is what your success will mean to the young ones in your world.

Have a kid, buy a condo

Let me share a personal example of the have a kid, buy a condo strategy. I have two little kids, and when they were born, I began to think about things I had never considered before. The cost of diapers, the cost of nursery school, the *cost of college*! Go on the Web, as I did, and search for projections of what college will cost if you have a child today. Get your barf bag ready, because the only place left in America where there is no pressure to reduce costs is on college campuses. Last time I checked, it was more than $250,000 to educate one child, and that's not including post-graduate degrees. So unless your little spawn are super athletes or a super geniuses, you are going to either have to come up with a pile of cash in a few years, or saddle them with a major debt burden.

When confronted with this reality, I naturally turned to the asset class I trust and understand best—real estate investment. I found the simplest investment I could for this purpose: a small condo on the outskirts of the New York City suburbs. Newburgh, New York, is a about an hour and a half from Manhattan, and represents just about the best value in real estate prices for people who work in or around New York City. The rental market there is reasonably strong, because there are not many large apartment complexes for a little landlord like me to compete with. There are most likely markets near you that fit this profile as well.

I located a small condo that was priced at $200,000 and bought it back in 2002, when my daughter was a year old. It didn't take long for my real estate agent to find me a tenant, and the seed was planted.

Making that commitment at such an early stage enabled me to set a long term maturity date on that investment. I had a clear objective for the investment; to have $250,000 available for college in 18 years, when the little munchkin graduates high school.

If you compare this to a college savings plan, you will find that you would have to sock away almost $1,000 a month for 18 years in order to have the cash available for college, which requires incredible discipline. It's more discipline than I and most people I know have. Every once in a while, finances get tight. An unexpected home repair, car repair, or other expenditure causes people to miss installments into a savings plan, or put the plan on hold until "things improve." Consider how a college savings plan compares to a real estate investment during a painful recession. Would most people have the fortitude to continue a long-term savings plan that requires a monthly installment of $1,000? Probably not.

But my real estate investment was locked in. I have a mortgage that must be paid, and tenants that pay it. There wasn't a moment during the housing crisis that I contemplated selling that condo. I never, for one second, worried about declining real estate values or thought about liquidating. There was no chance I was going to flake out.

It was never intended to be a "buy and flip." It was not about making short-term money. It is all about $250,000 in 2020.

One of the most interesting characteristics of this investment strategy is how the passion for the objective (educating my baby girl) made me so patient, tolerant, and energized to handle the periodic hassles that come with being a landlord.

When the phone call comes in from my tenant, telling me she's leaving at the end of next month, I have to go through the whole rigmarole of contacting my local broker, getting the property cleaned up, and placing it on the market for rent. I have to drive up there and inspect it. I have to bring the carpet cleaners in, look for holes in the walls, get the place tidied up, freshly painted, and ready for the next tenant. I have to hire the broker to market that property. You could do it yourself, but I choose to use a broker because I'm confident in the people that I have in the local markets. They'll find me a tenant relatively quickly, but then I have to pay a commission. I also have to meet the new tenants, and pray that new tenant is going to be as good as the old tenant at paying her rent on time.

The hassles of being a landlord are not confined to the times when there is a change in tenancy. The calls come in periodically that the washer and dryer are broken, or the roof is leaking, and I have to make a bunch of phone calls to handle the problem.

The funny thing is, I don't mind. People are so afraid of being a landlord because of the details I describe here, but when the work is connected to a goal that is so close to your heart, you just don't mind. When the phone rings and I see the caller ID is from my tenant, I don't cringe. I think about Diana. It's the same when I get a call from the tenant who is living in Patrick's college fund. This is for my kids.

15 | THE SNOWBALL

The biggest risk in writing a book on real estate investing is that I could become branded as one of "those guys." You know, the late-night cable, sitting on my yacht with champagne, shouting about how you too can get rich in real estate. When writing this book, I was given some pretty pointed advice that, in order to sell a book on real estate, it has to be about getting rich quick. "People are too impatient," "They don't have the attention span." Fair enough. I need immediate gratification as much as anyone.

The right way to get immediate gratification is to set your long-term plan so firmly in place that it frees you up to focus on making a short-term score. Once you've created a strategy that anchors your investment plan to long-term objectives, it is safe then to think in terms of making money *now*.

I learned at a young age that it was useless to try and change myself. I liked who I was, even though I could be impulsive, excitable, and prone to leaping before I looked. The first financial advisor I ever worked with gave me some great advice. He said, "Build your financial plan like a pyramid. Start at the bottom with the boring responsible things, add a layer that takes a little more risk and has growth potential, *and blow the rest.*" Spend it all! It's not reckless if you take care of the foundation first.

You have to love that last part. The theory is that a plan that relies on exerting discipline is less likely to succeed than a plan that plays into a human being's desire to live it up. No matter how much I had in my pocket after the basic investments got made each month, I was spending it. Over time, we just kept increasing the amounts I had to sock away, but my eye was always on the prize, kind of like eating your green beans because it qualifies you for dessert.

The theory applies to real estate investing because you have to give yourself little victories along the way, or it could get boring.

The biggest mistake people make in real estate is selling in order to realize the profit. They don't see it on paper as money in the bank and feel a burning desire to turn the hard asset back into a liquid asset. Don't do that! Equity in real estate is, for all intents and purposes, liquid. You need a few months to get to it, either by selling or by taking a cash-out refinance, but it's your money. Let it stay where it is until you have another real estate play to make, or your objective has been met and its time to liquidate.

Many investors do what I call a snowball strategy. They only ever hold one property at a time, but they make multiple acquisitions during a longer period of time by selling the last property and rolling the equity into the next.

For example, many people start thinking about where they want to retire decades in advance. It makes for good daydreaming material and vacation conversation. Once you choose the place you want to retire, it's a great idea to buy an entry-level piece of real estate and plant your seed. You can stay there when you go on vacation and rent it out for the rest of the season, or rent it year-round and stay somewhere else while on vacation. Either way, you are building momentum and equity in that place, and chances are, if you love it enough to want to retire there, you are not alone. You represent a migration trend that will help insure the future value of your investment.

It's kind of like how Warren Buffet picks stocks. He is known for being a value investor. He buys stock in companies that make products he likes. It's the same thing.

A few years after buying your entry-level property, sell it and roll it up into the next property, and so on and so on, until you retire. This is a great plan for several reasons:

1. The scenario establishes the direct connection of an investment with a passionate, long-term goal.

2. You become a specialist in this market. You get the local news-paper and keep tabs on what's happening with great interest. There will be no surprises because you are on top of it. It is not homework. It's a hobby that you enjoy.

3. The element of short-term gratification is present because you make several deals along the way.

4. You have multiple opportunities to add value. Each deal can create additional equity because you are always trolling for a good opportunity. Maybe an acquaintance wants to sell and you are able to get a good price in a private sale, or you scout foreclosures until something turns up, or you get in on a pre-construction deal, or you buy a vacant lot and build the home of your dreams efficiently.

A snowball strategy that turns a vacation home into a retirement home is a very reliable way to use real estate for retirement, and it's a ton of fun.

Professional investors who have large portfolios will often structure their portfolio into a series of snowballs. Compartmentalization is a very important principle in this business. They will often choose several local markets to take positions in, but it's only one position at a time in each locale. They find a place they believe is going to grow at a greater rate than the market, such as where a major retailer is moving, or a university is growing, and they buy their first property. They keep their ears to the ground in that market now, as a natural outgrowth of having made an investment there, and when the next gem comes along, they sell the prior property and roll the equity, and maybe additional capital, into the next. One client who liked this approach started with a three-family house, rolled into a six-family building, then rolled into a strip mall with 12 stores. During a 12-year period, he amassed $2 million in equity from an initial investment of $50,000. This was technically a long-term strategy because he bought and held in the market, but he didn't hold specific properties. Instead, he found three opportunities to create value, and therefore profited at a much greater rate than the market overall.

16 | THE LAW OF PROXIMITY

"There's a house on your street for sale!
Buy it or someone else will!"

—Kui Pak

Kui Pak is a real estate agent who worked in our brokerage years ago. Kui (pronounced Kay) is a great
guy. He is a Korean immigrant who speaks broken
English, which makes selling real estate a little challenging,
but he found a niche.

Back before selling foreclosures was fashionable, Kui became a "HUD Certified Agent," which means he went through a training and screening process that allowed him to represent buyers who were purchasing foreclosed properties that were owned by the U.S. Department of Housing and Urban Development. These were FHA government-insured loans that went bad.

Each week, he would get a fax from HUD listing the foreclosures, if any, that were being put on the market in his area. Then he would call all the other houses on the block and tell whoever answered the phone, *"There's a house on your street for sale! Buy it or someone else will!"*

He had a tremendously high hit rate with this approach, becoming a top producer in the company. He understood one of the most basic rules of real estate investing: proximity.

Buying an investment on your street is the greatest way to mitigate the risks and hassles of being a landlord. Maintaining a property on your block is easier because you are right there. Now, instead of maintaining one lawn on Maple Street, you maintain two. Instead of one kitchen to maintain appliances in, you have two. Now you shovel two driveways, but they are across the street from each other. It is almost like not being a property manager at all, but just having a bigger house to maintain.

Rent collection is also easier. Your tenants are familiar with you, and can't easily duck you if they are behind on rent. Knocking on their door to collect rent doesn't carry with it the dread that you are on someone else's turf. This is your block. Your confidence is boosted.

You are also literally a resident expert. Who knows more about this particular investment than you? Distance creates the potential for surprises. Conversely, close proximity ensures that you know the market intimately. Compare this level of expertise with buying a stock. There are thousands of professional traders who have better trading tools than you, more experience, and the ability to pay full-time attention to the market. You, as an amateur investor, can not compete with those traders. You are outgunned.

On your street, you are the big dog. You send your kids to the schools, you shop in the grocery store. You walk the block. There is no one who is more knowledgeable than you, with the exception of your neighbors. And like Kui Pak said, if you don't buy, one of them probably will.

17 | Own Where You Live, Own Where You Work

If you are a business owner, you know that there are very few things you can count on. One of them is that you will have a line item on your budget called "rent" and it's one of the big ones. With the exception of home-based businesses, they all need to be located somewhere. You need to own that location.

Acquiring the real estate where you operate your business is a natural strategy that hits on all the fundamental elements of a successful real estate strategy. Unless you are a 22-year-old entrepreneur who is appalled by the notion of having to wait until you're 30 years old to be wealthy, you are probably envisioning your business to be a long-term effort. Careers as a business owner run their course within 20 to 40 years. Somewhere along the way, buy a building. This may sounds obvious, but there are some forces that keep business owners from doing it. Let me illustrate with an example.

My father was a doctor who started a small medical practice in Nyack, New York back in the early 1970s. Like all start-ups, he began in a small rental space. After a few years, a small, plain house came on the market less than a mile from Nyack Hospital, which is where his patients stayed when they were sick.

He bought the little house on the side of the road and turned it into his medical office. Then he went about his life; raising kids, building his practice, contributing to the community. Twenty years went by in a flash. Along the way, some pretty swanky office buildings went up nearby that were designed to serve the doctors in the area, and many of his colleagues jumped in. You know the type: glass buildings, beautiful landscaping, marble lobbies, state-of-the-art telecommunications. It was a prestigious move for a doctor to relocate there, but not Dad. He likes his little office. He would grow tomatoes in the backyard, sit on the patio and rest between patient visits, and pay the mortgage instead of the landlord.

He resisted the temptation to rent a sweeter space, and chose to own the place where he worked. When he retired, that thing was paid off. On his last day in private practice, he sold that building and got one last paycheck. It contributed greatly to his ability to retire comfortably.

Here is another example from a recent closing of a client. An attorney with a small private practice ran his business out of a small, nondescript building in a quiet suburban community. He was a small-town lawyer who too often gave away his services to needy clients who could not pay. The way he put it was, "I am a good lawyer, but a lousy business man."

In the end, he did not grow a practice with other partners and associates. It was just him, his wife (who was the paralegal), and one administrator. He had not built shareholder value. There was nothing to sell once he retired. He did, however, buy the ugly ducking building 30 years earlier.

Was this a life-altering decision? You bet it was. His law firm was not worth anything without him running it, but on his final day of practicing law, he sold the building and received a $650,000 check at the closing. His life in retirement was altered from a life of worry to a life of financial security.

At that closing was another attorney, age 32, who was making the same life-altering decision to buy that same building, and set up his private practice there. At the end of the closing, the seller handed over the keys to the buyer with a tear in his eye, and said, "take care of her and she will take care of you."

The new owner gave the building a total makeover, and with enormous pride, has renewed the building's life cycle for another 30 years, at which time it will likely be adopted by a new owner and start the cycle again.

18 | DISTRESSED PROPERTY

This is where your once-in-a-generation opportunity exists. You've read the headlines "4,000,000 foreclosures," "3,000,000 short sales," "one in every four borrowers underwater on their mortgages," "Walk away from your mortgage!"

For reasons described previously, there are many pieces of property that are being taken back by the banks from homeowners who can not pay their mortgage obligations. These are commonly referred to as "distressed properties."

Some people get squeamish when we talk about a distressed property because they feel the property owner is in pain, and capitalizing on someone else's pain is wrong. I don't disagree with that conclusion, but nothing in *Crash Boom!* depends on someone else's pain. When you've seen as many real estate transactions close-up as I have, you learn that the buyer of a distressed property is providing the *solution* to the problem. He didn't create the distress. The responsible parties and actions are in the past. The bank owns it now and needs to sell it. You are the solution. If you are the highest bidder on a property at the time when a seller needs to sell, you are helping him. Don't lose sight of this fact.

Here is the key to the unprecedented opportunity before you. The housing market has already corrected itself by the time of this writing. It has already given back about 30 percent of its value from the peak (on the national scale). That represents the *only* time property values have decreased nationally since the Great Depression, when values also declined 30 percent. After the Great Depression, the positive economic cycles and the periodic recessions that followed led to a 60-year period of real estate appreciation! The market over-corrected during the Great Depression. It is about to again.

We are at a point where the values are flattening out at the appropriate post-correction levels, but values are likely to drop again in the next few years as a result of the second wave of the foreclosure crisis hitting the market. There is a stockpile of aggressively priced real estate coming to a town near you during the next few years. Those properties are going to be priced to sell quickly, because the sheer volume is unprecedented and the banks can't carry them any longer than necessary. You may have heard about the shadow inventory on the news. This refers to a supply of foreclosed homes that will be hitting the market as the banks take them back from defaulting homeowners. It is an inventory of properties in the shadows. This is the gold rush of our generation.

Let's say you have already found your Florida. You've researched and picked a winning market based on solid fundamentals and great future prospects. Now it's time to pick a winning property from the shadow inventory as it shows itself.

There are several categories of distressed properties for potential investors. Most of them fall somewhere along the timeline of a property being foreclosed upon.

Short Sale

When a homeowner seeks to sell a property that is "underwater" (mortgage balance exceeds value), the resulting transaction is called a short sale. In this instance, the homeowner and the bank are working together to dispose of the property *without* a costly and painful foreclosure. Properties listed for sale with realtors will normally be flagged as short sales. The homeowners are "short," and don't care so much what the house sells for because they are walking away from the closing with no money. The bank cares, but the bank is overwhelmed with cases of short sales and foreclosures. They often make snap decisions, which can mean you get an outstanding price. Completing a short sale requires a buyer to be ready with cash or financing, make a strong offer with minimal contingencies (strings attached), and promise a fast closing. Your communication with the bank's Loss Mitigation Department will be long and frustrating. Expect them to take *at least* 60–90 days to make a decision, but when they do, you will have bought a property at an under-market price. It is very important to use a real estate agent who is experienced in selling property in short sale situations. Experienced agents are patient and know how to deal with the bank personnel.

Pre-foreclosure

REO.com, RealtyTrac.com and Realquest.com are all subscription-based Websites that have foreclosure data on most markets around the country. For a reasonable monthly fee, users can browse local markets and receive data gleaned from the public record on all foreclosure filings. These are situations where a foreclosure process has begun, but the homeowner still owns the property. It is a distressed situation, and the solution is a ready, willing, and able buyer to make the best bid. In normal times, you might expect a lot of competition by other buyers for these properties, but because there are so many homes in pre-foreclosure now, that is not always the case.

Real Estate Owned (REO)

These are true foreclosures; properties that have been taken back by the bank. Lenders with inventories of properties they have already foreclosed on and taken possession of will work with third-party agencies to dispose of (sell) the properties. Those agencies usually have a local real estate broker handling the sales at the local level.

There are usually just a few brokers who specialize in REO in each area. Find out who they are and reach out to them. By making contact with an REO specialist, you can get on a short list of investors they will send a note to when a new list of REO inventory hits the market. Become a client of theirs and they will give you a heads-up that could be all the edge you need.

Distressed Condition

Sometimes the distress is not a financial matter, but one of physical condition. One of the easiest ways to increase the value of a property is to fix it up. Look at it another way. Sometimes the best way to get a great price is to buy a property no one else wants because it is a dump. One man's trash is another man's treasure.

Distressed Market

We've already discussed how Florida is a state in distress, for now. There are many places, unfortunately, that experience periods of decline or decay. Maybe a major employer moved out or closed. Maybe the area is overly dependent on an industry that is downsizing. It can be no more complicated than a tough neighborhood that is changing for the better.

Finding a distressed property is all about doing your homework, digging, using your intuition, and trusting your gut.

Business Journals

Most areas have a local or county-wide business journal, and they probably have an online component to them. Those publications are dedicated to reporting on the economic trends in their territory with very specific examples. To find a local business journal, search Google. For example "Charleston S.C. Business Journal" returned the following:

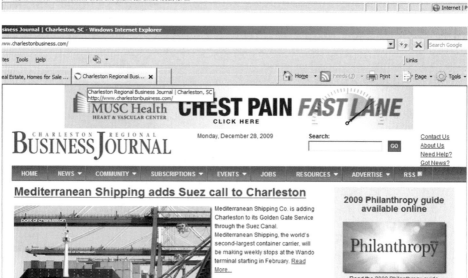

These publications exist in virtually every metropolitan area, or county. They are dedicated to reporting on the economic development activity in the area, such as a new employer moving in or out. The headline alone tells you that the shipping business in Charleston (the city's main industry) is growing.

- Is the University adding a wing? Or are they experiencing a downturn in their student population?

- Are the major employers doing well? Are they hiring, firing, acquiring, or being acquired?

- Is Walmart coming in alongside Kmart? Is Home Depot already there, and will Lowes be moving in? Or are these well-researched retailers staying away?

- What is the governmental climate for business? Does the local market have an Economic Development Agency, or Business Association working with the local, regional, or state government in attracting new business with services and incentives?

Anytime someone who has more capital at risk than you chooses to place a bet on an area, that's a very good sign. When someone with more experience in choosing markets with good long-term prospects, and more resources to research opportunities makes a move, you should consider following in their footsteps.

U.S. Census

Population trends are the biggest of the big picture. Are the experts projecting the population in an area will grow, shrink, or stay the same in 10 to 20 years? How does that compare to other nearby or related areas?

Choosing a winning market can be as simple as looking at the population trends, because there are reasons why population grows and why people are attracted to some areas instead of others, such as:

- Proximity to jobs.

- Transportation.

- Quality of life.

- Access to the city.

- Taxation.

- Politics.

- Crime.

- Schools.

- Branding and marketing by the localities.

- Scenic beauty.

- Cost of living.

- Density.

- Climate.

Every one of these is important to the long-term health of a real estate market, and understanding the long-term population trends can tie them all together in one measurement. People vote with their feet. If a population is growing, this is a good thing because they need somewhere to live. Either they will be your tenant and pay you rent, or they will be another prospective buyer bidding for your property when you decide to sell.

To find the U.S. Census reports for a region, visit *www.census.gov*. There is a multitude of charts and reports available and you can select a state, county, or town and see local trends such as population change, household income change, and so on. You can also visit OwnAmerica. com for links to population resources.

What is the average population growth in the last 10 years in the United States? Is Tennessee growing faster or slower than the rest of the nation? Also, is income per household growing or shrinking? Is Nashville growing faster or slower than the rest of the state?

Population trends = real estate demand in the future.

Income trends = the value of real estate in the future.

Planning Board Meetings

The way real estate is developed, whether by private industry, government, or non-profits, is all determined and negotiated at the local level. In virtually every market in this country, the local municipality, not the state or federal government, has jurisdiction over who, when, and how to put a shovel in the ground to develop real estate.

Each proposed project, whether it's a new apartment building, shopping center, office building, wing on the hospital, highway exit, or school, requires approval from the local body charged with that oversight. In most places, they are called the Planning Board. They hold regular public meetings in town to review plans and proposals for all potential developers. Go to the website of your town or city and look for the schedule. Show up, sit in the back, and watch what goes down.

Look for indications that other people are placing bets on this market, such as a new retail store, hotel, or residential development. Those people do their homework, and the bank they are borrowing money from does its homework as well. Even if you don't speak to them directly, you can watch their project unfold and get a sense of their confidence in the market. The details of their proposals are often public record, so their research can become your research.

By attending these meetings, you will bear witness to the governmental attitude towards business. Politicians may say they are "pro business" in their campaign speeches, but the rubber meets the road with the planning board. As described previously, sometimes a planning board is made of up people with way too much time on their hands, and a penchant for controlling the actions of others.

Much can be learned about the future of a town by attending its planning board meetings.

Housing Market Data

Understanding the market cycle is not a national endeavor. Each local market has its own cycle. The curve of a local cycle will almost always mimic the state-wide cycle and the national cycle, but it will never be identical. Herein you will find another opportunity to pick a winner. Following are 10-year charts showing the median sale price in that market through the current cycle.

The following charts were generated easily on OwnAmerica.com.

MEDIAN SALE PRICE - USA
September 2000 - August 2010

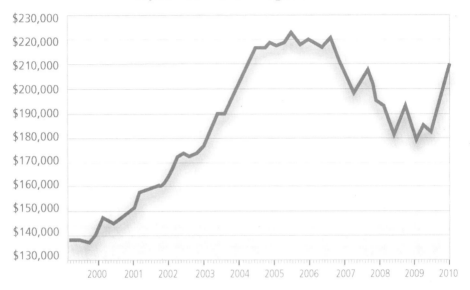

OwnAmerica.com

U.S. Market

Started low, peaked, corrected, and is close to bottoming out. You can make observations on the fly with this chart. You know what happened in 2001 that made the housing market dip. You know what it was like in 2003 and 2004 when things were booming. You felt the crest of the curve and then the decline. Now you are feeling the leveling off.

In other words, reconcile your personal experience, and what you know about recent history to explain the ups and downs of this chart.

Then look at other markets and see what you can glean by doing the same analysis, and comparing one local market to another, or to the state or nation.

MEDIAN SALE PRICE - Cleveland Metro
September 2000 - August 2010

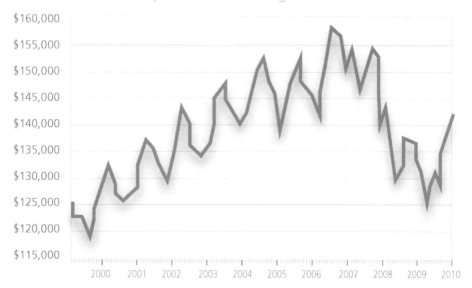

OwnAmerica.com

Cleveland, Ohio

Started low, peaked, tumbled all the way down to almost the original low from the beginning of the cycle. Cleveland is now leveling off. This is a stable market whose highs are not too high, and lows are not too low. Cleveland is a place you can find a winning property for a very affordable buy-in price and pay it down over time with very little risk. This kind of chart would necessitate a deeper look into the Cleveland economy to explain the drop in value. It is most likely related to the decline in manufacturing in Ohio.

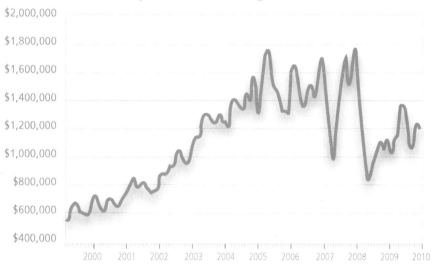

MEDIAN SALE PRICE - Laguna Beach
September 2000 - August 2010

OwnAmerica.com

Laguna Beach, California

Part of the boom market in California. The numbers started fairly high, and went crazy. Much of the peak appreciation has burned off in the correction, but the real dollars of gain during 10 years are astounding. This market has a high barrier of entry because the prices are high, but it's Pacific Ocean waterfront.

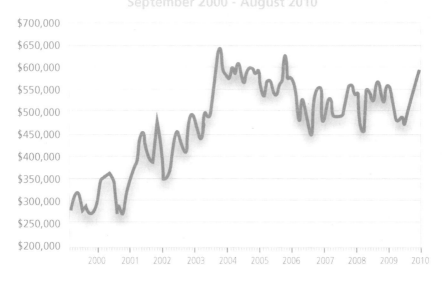

MEDIAN SALE PRICE - White Plains
September 2000 - August 2010

OwnAmerica.com

White Plains, New York

A suburb of Manhattan is almost as good as being on the Pacific Ocean. The robust job market of the Big Apple provides a blanket of security for the real estate markets nearby. Here the prices started pretty high, almost tripled, corrected, and stabilized quickly. After doing the homework described in this chapter, you would know that this was a market with many positive local trends supporting it.

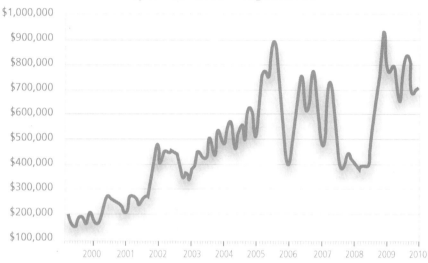

Palm Beach, Florida

Palm Beach is front and center in the trends that placed Florida at the top of the list of markets with short-term pain and long-term gain. Prices began this decade below $200,000 and got as high as $1 million before the peak, then went on a roller coaster ride. Did you hear about the mad overdevelopment, speculation, and lending? Here is the chart. If you ignore the peak, you see the real trend—steady and upward.

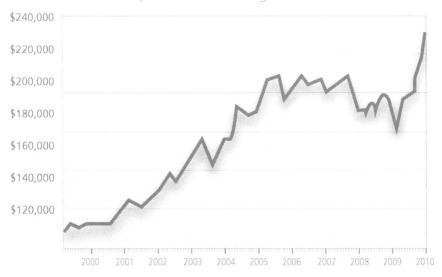

MEDIAN SALE PRICE - Charleston Metro
September 2000 - August 2010

OwnAmerica.com

Charleston, South Carolina

Starts low and mimics the national market curve. The migration trend that is driving Baby Boomers from the Northeast to Florida is driving Floridians to the Carolinas. As you can see, there was no housing meltdown in Charleston.

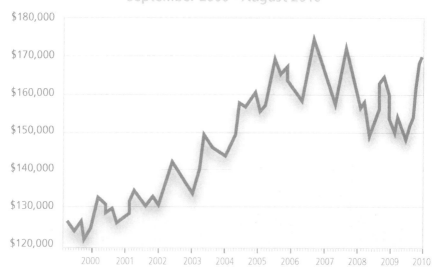

MEDIAN SALE PRICE - Nashville Metro
September 2000 - August 2010

OwnAmerica.com

Nashville, Tennessee

Here is a market that played to its own fiddler during this decade. The appreciation was not meteoric, so the correction was modest, and the leveling off was in-step with the overall curve. Ten years from now, I expect this curve to look straight, as if the "boom and crash" of the Roaring 2000s never happened.

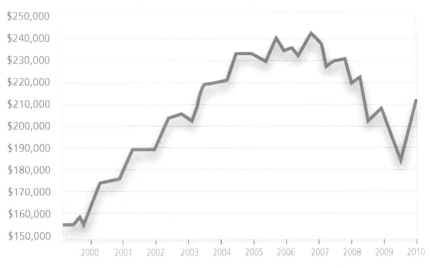

MEDIAN SALE PRICE - Minneapolis St. Paul Metro
September 2000 - August 2010

OwnAmerica.com

St. Paul, Minnesota

Another market that followed the national trend closely. Prices increased 120 percent from low to peak, and has since given back most of the gains. Median sale prices in St. Paul are at 2002 levels. This is a safe, solId market with a reasonable buy-in price.

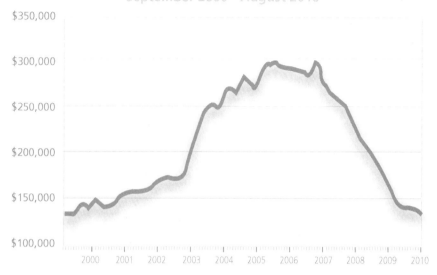

MEDIAN SALE PRICE - Las Vegas Metro
September 2000 - August 2010

Las Vegas, Nevada

The ultimate gambler's market. Over-development for a population that isn't there has caused Las Vegas to give back every penny of its gains from the beginning of the cycle. This is an example of a supply and demand situation that was out of whack. Too much supply, not enough demand, and no patience. The development trend in Las Vegas mirrored what happened in South Florida—massive new luxury development up and down the strip, as well as on the outskirts of town. Most of this development was residential, but the migration trends to Las Vegas are not as locked in as they are to Florida. California continues to migrate to Nevada, so the long-term prospects for Las Vegas are strong, but be patient.

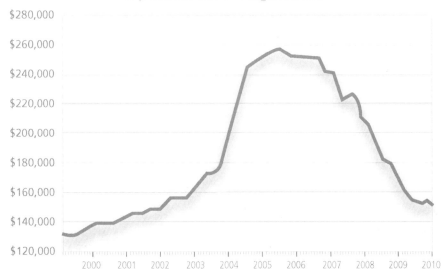

MEDIAN SALE PRICE - Phoenix Metro
September 2000 - August 2010

Phoenix, Arizona

A similar story to Las Vegas. Like other markets of this sort, the population trends didn't support the rabid development and speculation. Many investors lost their shirts because they bought at the peak of this curve. Now it's a new day for a new crop of investors. The ones who buy to hold and wait 10 years will do well.

• • • • •

Each chart has lows and highs that are different. The points of inflection (when changes in direction occur) are different, and the actual dollar amounts are different, but the general shape is strikingly similar. This is the heartbeat of the housing market, and the most important common denominator of most these markets is that the end point of a 10-year period is higher than the starting point.

19 | THE BUFFET
IS OPEN

To really understand the opportunity before you, you need to open your scope and grasp that real estate in not an investment option, but an entire field of business and entrepreneurship. If you internalize the fundamentals of buying wisely and riding the cycle, you can then unleash your creativity on the where, what, and why of your investment strategy. We've talked about finding markets that are on the ascendancy, and how they will lift all boats in the harbor. We've also talked about strategies to get an added lift by finding undervalued properties that are selling for below-market for a variety of reasons, and then ways to add even more value by altering the property in some way to make it more valuable. There are many dials you can turn up simultaneously to get more bang for your buck, and more bucks in your portfolio.

The possibilities are endless, but the property types fall into a few basic categories. The better you understand the types and their respective advantages and challenges, the better you can figure out which one(s) fit your personal profile and objectives.

Single-Family Homes

According to the U.S. Census, of the 112 million occupied housing units in America, 37 million of them are occupied by renters. And 32 percent of those are renting single-family homes; the most basic housing unit. That's more rental households than all the large apartment buildings in the country combined. This is due to two factors: single family homes make up most of the housing structures in America, and most people are hard-wired to want their space.

I like single-family homes as a fundamental investment unit because most people understand it. They are familiar because they may have grown up in one or live in one now. Familiarity breeds confidence, and confidence will lead to taking action. Remember, this book was designed to change your life (by compelling you to buy at least one piece of real estate and pay it off). Don't feel the need to overcomplicate this. As the Census shows, tenants love single-family homes.

Property management is fairly simple: one roof, one furnace, one dishwasher, one tenant. The neighborhoods are usually completely residential and are mostly made up of homeowners, so vandalism is not tolerated, and taxpayers are on the scene. It's more likely to be a safe, stable, and well-kept neighborhood.

The downside in single-family home investment is cash flow. One tenant often means it is harder to cover the monthly mortgage, taxes, and insurance. When you do your analysis, you will see that rents do not always keep up with costs of ownership, so it could be a negative cash flow investment in the beginning. However, in a few years, when the rents are increased, and your mortgage payment remains the same, single-family homes that start negative will become positive cash flow. This is why it is so important to use analysis tools that allow you to combine the factors of appreciation, amortization, *and* cash flow into one Internal Rate of Return. In fact, negative-cash-flow properties can product outstanding returns, even if you have to carry them for a few years and make up a shortfall between rent and costs.

Think of it in the context of other investment options. There is no such thing as a mutual fund that you don't have to put money into. Retirement plans such as 401ks and IRAs require that *you* write checks on a regular basis in order to build up a stash. Otherwise, the balance stays at zero and they just stop sending you statements. You think of it as an investment, and so you expect to invest. Approach real estate with the same expectation.

A negative-cash-flow real estate investment will require that you not only put up cash when you buy it, but also put up some as you season it. Let me illustrate with the condo I bought for my daughter's college fund. That condo cost me $1,800 a month to carry and I only got $1,550 a month in rent for the first two years, and then upped it to $1,700. It wasn't until the next tenant that I was able to get the number up high enough to cover the costs. But I didn't care. It's an investment, not a job. I didn't buy it to provide me with current income. I bought it to commit myself to a plan that would pay for her education 18 years later. Now it's positive cash flow and I still really don't care. I am not jumping for joy over the $150 I make each month. I am jumping for joy because college tuition isn't a concern for me.

This is an important point because too many investors reject negative cash flow properties that are awesome investments because they believe it *must* make current income on day one or it is a bad investment. Not so. My negative cash flow condo has produced an 11-percent annual return since I bought it, when you include appreciation and amortization in the equation. Show me a super low-risk mutual fund that does that.

Another reason I am tolerant of negative cash flow in the beginning is that current income is not as important as value. If you find a single-family home with three bedrooms plus a home office in an area where three-bedroom houses sell for $400,000 and four-bedroom houses sell for $500,000, you are going to convert that office into a fourth bedroom and add instant equity. If you also bought it from the bank after foreclosure, you got a good price. If you also learned that the nearby university is expanding, you have yourself a winner. Don't disqualify that investment when you learn that the rent is going to be a few hundred less than the expenses. This is still a smart buy because you have reasons to believe rents will rise. We are in the down cycle now, but we know what comes next.

This is not to say single-family homes are always negative cash flow investments, but the positive cash flow ones are harder to come by. I would rather find one with the previously described potential than one that I am buying at market value but breaks even. I have a job for income. This is about wealth.

Two- to Four-Family Homes

These are an incredibly appealing property type. For one thing, they do generate a profit on day one much more often. It makes sense. You have two, three, or four tenants paying you rent. It's almost universally true that you can generate more rental income from two 1,500-square-foot apartments in one building than you can from a 3,000-square-foot, single-family house. Smaller apartments typically carry a higher rent per square foot than larger ones.

Of course, property management is made more complicated by a factor of two, three, or four. You have more rent to collect, and that means more potential for someone to be late. You have more dishwashers that can break, and more people to yell at you when the roof leaks. You also have more apartments to keep occupied, which means extra paperwork, more conversations with your real estate agent, and so on. There is an upside to that, however. If you have three tenants and one leaves, you are still collecting rent from two others. With a single-family home, when your tenant leaves, you are out of business until you get another one.

There are also two powerful trends that make two- to four-family homes a great investment right now. The first trend is related to rental demand. Homeownership is trending downward. Since the peak in 2006, fewer people are buying homes, and an unprecedented number are losing their homes to foreclosure. Demand for rentals is way up. According to Harvard's Joint Center for Housing Studies, 800,000 new rental households were created in 2009 alone. And the kind of rentals most of them want comes with a backyard. They can't own a house, but they still want to live in one. Demand for apartments in large buildings is way down, replaced by demand for rentals in houses: single-, two-, three-, and four-family houses.

The second trend is related to supply. The entire home building industry was obsessed with building the same type of property during the past decade: luxury single-family homes or "McMansions." According to Harvard, construction of two- to four-family houses practically ceased to exist for the entire decade. This means that a property type that was already in short supply is even more rare now. As demand to rent these properties increases, and supply of new ones is practically non-existent, I see a very bright future of high rents and increased value for multi-family dwellings.

Find a multi-family foreclosure in a town that is not in decline, and you've found yourself a winner.

Mixed-Use Properties

You know the type. A store downstairs, and two or three apartments upstairs. These quaint buildings were the most popular form of downtown construction for a few hundred years in America. Then they went out of style when quaint went out of style in the 1950–1970s. Now everyone realizes that charm matters, and they are back.

Mixed-use properties have all the benefits and challenges of a typical two- to four-family house: more work and more income. But there are a couple of extra benefits and wrinkles to a mixed use.

First, you have a commercial tenant downstairs. This adds diversity to your roster of tenants. They pay higher rents, almost always higher than a residential tenant, and many commercial tenants want to secure their location, so they want longer leases. Three-year leases are as typical as 10-year leases. Once you sign them, you keep getting paid, unless they go out of business.

Mixed-use properties are more susceptible to loss of income in a recession. Businesses fold up in hard times. But mixed-use buildings are less susceptible than, say, a small office building where *all* the tenants are businesses.

Second, location is king. Chances are that mixed-use properties exist on streets such as Broadway and Main Street. You just don't get any more central than that. Of course, not every downtown is on its way up, or even stable. This is where your big picture research on population trends, governmental attitudes toward business, demographics, job market stability, and so on will keep you out of trouble. We've all seen ghost towns. You don't want to buy in a ghost town unless you know revitalization is afoot. If, however, you identify a quiet downtown that has better days ahead for tangible reasons, it becomes a very exciting movement to become part of. Just don't put all your eggs in one basket because sometimes turnarounds get turned around.

Commercial Real Estate

I am intentionally focusing on residential real estate for two reasons: First, the price points on commercial real estate are high and therefore out of reach for many independent investors, and secondly, the direct connection between population growth and housing does not exist with commercial real estate. Population grows, even during down economies.

Businesses usually do not grow during recessions. The cycle for commercial real estate is reliable but driven by economic trends, which are far more fickle than population trends.

Having said that, much of the strategy discussed in *Crash Boom!* applies to commercial real estate. In fact, many of the more advanced strategies were developed by commercial investors. Having had the privilege of working with and witnessing the genius of these professionals, I was able to boil them down and apply them to residential investment strategy. Adaptive re-use, for example, is a commercial real estate concept.

There are five general categories of commercial real estate that have different drivers, challenges, and opportunities. There is immense wealth that is created by investing in these property types.

Industrial

You see them on the way to the airport: factories and warehouses. These are highly complex buildings in their management, operation, financing, and tenant relations, and don't belong as an adjunct to a book on residential investing. I will only cover one interesting trend related to industrial real estate that can help you see some strategic parallels with residential.

In the mid 1800s, the western world entered an era that became known as the Industrial Revolution. The invention of mechanized tools and the processes to generate power with water, coal, and oil changed the world. It also created a need for a new infrastructure to house the plants, factories, and warehouses. No one had much inventory until we started building things with machines and piling up our supply. Whole areas around major cities and small towns were designated for industrial use, and buildings were erected. Some towns became "factory towns" where an industrialist would build a factory and support the entire local economy.

Just as everything changed when the industrial revolution enabled us to make things with machines, the Information Revolution changed everything again. Beginning in the 1970s, the American workforce and economy began to shift away from making things, and toward creating, designing, servicing, and distributing things. Not only has this had an epic effect on the workforce of the world, but on the industrial infra-structure in the United States. This can be devastating, as it has been to the states, cities, and towns that did the majority of the manufacturing during the last century. The states of Michigan and Ohio are still going through a painful reconditioning as those factories go dark.

The opportunity in industrial real estate is in the repurposing of some of the non-descript industrial buildings you might drive by all your life and never notice. If you play sports, or have kids that play sports and go to birthday parties, you have probably been inside a repurposed ware-house recently and may not be aware of it.

Indoor soccer, tennis, baseball, skating, and paint ball facilities and jumpy-castle birthday party places are being retrofitted from former warehouse buildings all over America these days. These buildings have large square footage open spaces with high ceilings and great parking. They are usually far too expensive to build for a sports/entertainment fa-cility to be able to afford, but they are often very reasonable rents. Ware-house space is normally the lowest price per square foot use of real estate in any area. Warehouses used to store paper towels, lumber, dishwashers, or gummy bears are low-rent buildings. When the former occupants left the building, and no new tenants were forthcoming, owners of warehouses everywhere began to see their property in a new light. They began to realize that their location off the beaten track is not a detriment to the sports/entertainment business. This is not a shoe store that needs high visibility, or a corporate office that needs a fancy address. It's a place that draws people to the other side of the tracks for the experience only a former warehouse can provide.

A perfect example of this exists in every populated area around the country where soccer and lacrosse have made a major resurgence. Years ago, little league was all about baseball. Fields were built next to schools and on municipal property in every town for America's pastime. Now soccer and lacrosse are getting to these kids at younger and younger ages. In fact, everyone I know with little kids is carting them all over creation every weekend, all year long. Kids play multiple organized sports, and leagues need places to practice and play. This is no short-term trend. These kids are hooked, and the high schools and colleges are loving the quality of the athletes that are showing up every year. Kids love it, parents love it, and coaches love it. It's not showing any signs of slowing down.

For the 25,000- to 100,000-square-foot warehouse, this new business trend is exactly what they needed to remain relevant and drive their value.

If buying a warehouse and converting it into a sports facility is not in your scope, you can still internalize the lesson. Zoom out and what do you see? The supply of these specially equipped buildings is very limited.

Demand is strong and growing. Try to book one of these places for a private party on a weekend. They are raking it in. The value of old warehouses is suppressed because the old use is no longer as relevant, and the old tenants paid low rent anyway. The big picture looks sweet because of this new purpose. Now you zoom in and find your winner.

Office buildings

Again, this is a high price point and a complex animal to master, so I will simply share some fundamentals and a trend to watch. Obviously, the office market is inextricably connected to the business economy. When business is bad, companies cut spending, and the two biggest items on their budget are payroll and rent. If unemployment is up, chances are, so are office vacancies. There is an interesting opportunity to acquire office buildings that are impacted in a special way by this particular recession. As you may know, this recession was debt-driven. We hear about it more from the consumer perspective (people being underwater on homes or maxed our of credit cards) and from the government perspective (they are heaping debt onto our grandchildren!), but there is a third rail of debt that caused this crisis: business debt.

Companies in all kinds of businesses, from banking, to insurance, to manufacturing and retail began inventing a new business model in their fields. New sources of capital emerged from hedge funds and private equity firms that enabled businesses to create wealth by doing everything on credit. Here is how it might go for a retailer:

- Step 1—Buy $1 million worth of product on credit.

- Step 2—Sell the product for $2 million.

- Step 3—Pay the creditor.

- Step 4—Multiply by a factor of 10, or 50, and repeat.

The model works great until there is no one to buy the product and you owe the creditor more money than your company is worth. The result is flash-bankruptcy. Stick the keys in the door and walk away with whatever you can salvage. Out of business overnight.

This model has a variation that works in ownership of office buildings as well. Here is how it goes:

- Step 1—Buy a building for $100 million with a mortgage of $60 million.

- Step 2—Get a loan a few years later from a "new" lending source who would happily loan you 80 percent of the value, or $80 million.

- Step 3—Put the $20 million in your pocket, tax-free. Happy days are here again.

- Step 4—The loan is a "balloon" loan, which means you are required to pay it off in five years. This could be accomplished with a refinance or a sale of the building. But the recession brings the value of the building down to $75 million, and the "new" lenders are gone. All that's left are some of the old lenders, who only loan 60 percent of the value of the building.

$75 million X 60 percent = $45 million

Existing loan to be paid off = $80 million.

Shortfall = $35 million, which is more than the value of the company. Flash bankruptcy.

This is an example of distressed property on a grand scale. We are seeing great buildings, in perfect condition, with great tenants paying their rent, that are going bankrupt because this debt-driven business model hit a wall. The lesson is that the more you look around, the more you find changes that are creating opportunities. You also see people, even the smartest professional investors, lose when they ignore the fundamentals: Buy, hold, pay down.

20 | SEEING INTO THE FUTURE

While it's true that you can't count your chickens before they hatch, and you never count your money while you're sitting at the table, it's also true that it's a lot more fun to do exactly that. In case you haven't noticed, I am a big believer in taking a long-term approach to real estate investing. But I also believe that it's crucial to visualize your plan working, and take the time to dream about your life when you've achieved your outcome.

Technology exists today that allows you to see into the future and count those chickens. It is perfectly responsible to do so. In fact, it's the only way to truly understand the power of real estate as an investment and make the right decisions on what, where, and when to invest.

We've gone into detail about the core calculations of a real estate investment:

> Rental Income
>
> - Operating Expenses
>
> = Net Operating Income
>
> - Debt Service
>
> = Cash Flow

But that is a static calculation. It only tells you what is happening right now, and doesn't give you the ability to add the dimension of time to your analysis. Rents and expenses will change. The property will appreciate, and the mortgage balance will be reduced every month. Your true return on investment can't be calculated by a simple static formula. In order to see the result of a long-term real estate investment, you need to be able to incorporate appreciation and mortgage amortization to establish how much you have built in equity. Then add to that all the cumulative positive cash flow you've generated. Then that total net gain in wealth must be compared to all the money you actually invested, including your down payment and closing costs, capital improvements, and negative cash flow. In other words, if you want to know how this investment has performed, you need to know everything you've put out, everything you've brought in, and how the market has performed. Sounds complicated, but with today's technology, it's not.

A real estate investment can be boiled down to one number: Internal Rate of Return, which can then be compared to other investment options to allow you to judge how well you did. You will see that this asset class performs better than the others. Calculating Internal Rate of Return (IRR) 10 years into the future requires that you make assumptions about a half-dozen numbers, such as rents, expenses, and appreciation rate.

Future Value

Because history repeats itself in economics and the housing market, the best and only way to forecast the value of a property in the future is to look at the past. I am not saying you should look at how a property performed in the last five years and project that for the next five. I am saying that if you look back 20 years, which is well into the last cycle, you will see that the market reverts to a mean, or average appreciation rate. Again, you must zoom all the way out to see the trend, and when you do, you can't miss it.

Using the modern cycle as an example, at the time of this writing, the housing market in America has processed and eliminated the entire "bubble" that grew from 2002–2007. *Poof!* It's gone. Most regional markets are back to 2002 prices, and may go back further before this is all over. That is what's called an overcorrection, and it is setting us up for appreciation in the future. Watch the curves shoot up, and you can anticipate that they will come down. Watch them flatten for a while, and you know there is a revival on the way. When you average it all out, it ends up a little higher than inflation. Once you determine the average appreciation rate, you can use it as a baseline for what could happen in the future, and you can adjust up or down, depending on your market intelligence or general conservatism.

How do you do it? Until recently, you couldn't, but the availability of national housing data complete with historical records is now available at OwnAmerica.com. By simply choosing a zip code, you can see the history and get the number. For our case study, let's say the market appreciated at 3.5 per year during the last 20 years. This is *not* IRR. This is annual appreciation, and it's just the first assumption you must make to see the future.

The next one is simple; mortgage amortization. If you are buying with a mortgage, chances are you will need to make a 25-percent down payment as a minimum, so your beginning mortgage balance will be 75 percent of the value. Using a 30-year fixed-rate loan, you will then determine what the current mortgage rates are (also available at OwnAmerica.com).

The next piece of information needed is rental income. A local real estate advisor is always the best source of potential rental income for a property, but other sources exist to use as a baseline, to be verified by a local expert. Rentometer.com aggregates rental data from several apartment websites. It is useful as a source, but should not be relied upon exclusively.

Craigslist is another online source of rental information that can give a snapshot of asking rents for virtually every market in the county. Used in conjunction with MLS data and real-world experience, rental information is not difficult to gather and understand.

The best data you can get is from a local real estate agent who can pull up not just asking rents for available apartments, but what tenants have actually agreed to pay for recently rented units similar to your subject property. Your real estate agent will also give you a sense of how busy the rental market is and how many months it will likely take to rent it out. At that time, you make an estimate of your vacancy rate, and determine how much actual rent you will be collecting in the first year.

Operating expense should be verified whenever possible. Taxes, utility bills, insurance, lawn maintenance, and so on are simple to determine. Estimates can be used to fill in the blanks on things such as legal fees, repairs, and maintenance. Now you must estimate the increases in rent and expenses as a percentage. It is reasonable to use the rate of inflation, which has been hovering between 2 and 3 percent for 10 years. Be conservative.

Let's bring it all together. You have made educated guesses on how much your property will appreciate per year, how much rent you will collect, and expenses you will pay this year, and how much those will increase or decrease over time. You have also determined how much of a mortgage you will borrow, and how long that mortgage term is. You are now ready to plug these numbers into any number of readily available software solutions that will crunch all the numbers and show you:

1. How much equity you will have 10 or 15 years into the future as the property appreciates and the mortgage balance declines.

2. How much annual cash flow (or loss) you will generate each year.

3. What the cumulative impact of all of these numbers are, in the form of a Internal Rate of Return.

Of course this is an art, and not a science. There are no guarantees that the market will continue to perform the way it has historically, or that your calculations will be accurate. The exercise, however, is a critical learning process. You *must* take educated guesses and then compare your guesses to reality. As you analyze properties this way, you will also learn how much of an impact changes in these figures can affect the long-term outcome.

Some examples:

- Getting a high rent is of little benefit if your unit stays vacant for 5 extra months while you secure a tenant.

- Having a positive cash flow is fantastic, but it will not make for a good long-term investment if the property value does not appreciate because you paid too much.

- Buying low, finding an undervalued property, and making some efficient improvement to it can dramatically improve your long-term performance by starting you off ahead.

Use the tools at OwnAmerica.com to do the research and you will see how all the moving parts work together. Get this right, and you will build a fortune, because timing is everything, and the time is now.

Conclusion: Out Into the World You Go. Good Luck and Stay in Touch

At the time of this writing, the housing crisis of the Great Recession has caused people all over America to question whether real estate is the powerful wealth-creating market that is used to be. They look at the millions of people being harmed by a bad real estate market and begin to believe it is the market that's to blame. It isn't. But don't expect the responsible parties to step up and take the blame for their role.

What those parties, whether they be in Washington, on Wall Street, or on Main Street have shown us is that the

American housing market is misunderstood. Real estate investing can be done incorrectly. It's my sincere hope that at the end of this book you are not one of those who misunderstand the housing market, and that you can take what you've absorbed here and apply it to your own research. Use your own creativity to find those places that are on the rise, and those properties that are waiting for you to elevate their value. If this will be your first time investing in American real estate, you are in for a thrilling ride. The pride of ownership can't be described. And when each piece of property you acquire is connected in your heart and mind to a life goal that you want so badly, you have done it right.

I'll make one final reference to the tools we've built at OwnAmerica. com. There are people all around the country who are taking their first trip down the path of real estate ownership, and others who have done it before and have knowledge to share. The social interaction at OwnAmerica.com is designed to get the conversation started, so go there, find each other, and share your plans, fears, and excitement.

I wish you all the luck in the world, but you don't really need it as long as you have the know-how, the timing, and the courage to be a real estate entrepreneur during the greatest economic opportunity since the Great Depression.

Index

homes, single-family, 188-190

Hoover, Herbert, 24

House, Poor, 34

housing cycle, the six phases of the, 71

Housing market
crisis, 44-45
data, 174
median price, United States, 73, 74, 75, 88

housing meltdown, the anatomy of a, 47-53

housing, multiple-family, 191-192

Hudson Rivers Stage, 107-109

I

Income, 85, 94
annual gross, 96-97
measuring the source of, 131

Industrial, the U.S. Housing Market and Dow Jones, 89

intelligence, marketing, 113-126

interest-only loans, 92

international markets and their decline, 26

investing, you believe in real estate, 132-142

investment by gender, views of the best long-term, 130

iPods, 18

irrational pessimism, 18, 55

ISS 101-102

J

journals, business, 169

K

Kennedy,
John F., 56
Joseph P., 56
Teddy, 56

Kraft, 36

L

Ladies Home Journal, 24

landlord scoring system, 141

landlords four categories of, 140

Lehman Brothers, 58

lender amnesia, 50-51

"letter," the, 48

leverage, 85, 89-90

live, own where you, 161-169

loans, interest-only, 92

ABOUT THE AUTHOR

Greg Rand has been a real estate entrepreneur for his entire adult life and half of his childhood. He founded OwnAmerica because he believes in the power of American real estate to change people's lives for the better. The timing of this book and the launch of the company was a direct response to the Great Recession and the housing crisis at the center of it. OwnAmerica is a Website company, which was referenced several times in Crash Boom!, and it is also an education company, offering training programs to investors and real estate brokers on how to play the real estate market like a pro. Greg is partner in one of the largest full-service real estate companies in the country. He is a regular contributor on cable business news, and the host of Rand on Real Estate on WABC radio in New York. Greg, his wife, and their two children split their time between White Plains, New York, and Seabrook Island, South Carolina.